CAMINO REAL*

"In the middle of the journey of our life I came to myself in a dark wood where the straight way was lost."

CANTO I, DANTE's *Inferno*

*Use Anglicized pronunciation: *Cá*-mino *Ré*al

By TENNESSEE WILLIAMS

PLAYS

Baby Doll (a screenplay)
Camino Real
Cat on a Hot Tin Roof
Clothes for a Summer Hotel
Dragon Country
The Glass Menagerie
A Lovely Sunday for Creve Coeur
Small Craft Warnings
Stopped Rocking & Other Screenplays
A Streetcar Named Desire
Sweet Bird of Youth

THE THEATRE OF TENNESSEE WILLIAMS, VOLUME I
Battle of Angels, A Streetcar Named Desire, The Glass Menagerie

THE THEATRE OF TENNESSEE WILLIAMS, VOLUME II
The Eccentricities of a Nightingale, Summer and Smoke, The Rose Tattoo, Camino Real

THE THEATRE OF TENNESSEE WILLIAMS, VOLUME III
Cat on a Hot Tin Roof, Orpheus Descending, Suddenly Last Summer

THE THEATRE OF TENNESSEE WLLIAMS, VOLUME IV
Sweet Bird of Youth, Period of Adjustment, The Night of the Iguana

THE THEATRE OF TENNESSEE WILLIAMS, VOLUME V
The Milk Train Doesn't Stop Here Anymore, Kingdom of Earth (The Seven Descents of Myrtle), Small Craft Warnings, The Two-Character Play

THE THEATRE OF TENNESSEE WILLIAMS, VOLUME VI
27 Wagons Full of Cotton and Other Short Plays

THE THEATRE OF TENNESSEE WILLIAMS, VOLUME VII
In the Bar of a Tokyo Hotel and Other Plays

27 Wagons Full of Cotton and Other Plays
The Two-Character Play
Vieux Carré

POETRY

Androgyne, Mon Amour
In the Winter of Cities

PROSE

Collected Stories
Eight Mortal Ladies Possessed
Hard Candy and Other Stories
The Knightly Quest and Other Stories
One Arm and Other Stories
The Roman Spring of Mrs. Stone
Where I Live: Selected Essays

CAMINO REAL

by TENNESSEE WILLIAMS

A NEW DIRECTIONS BOOK

FOR ELIA KAZAN

FOREWORD*

It is amazing and frightening how completely one's whole being becomes absorbed in the making of a play. It is almost as if you were frantically constructing another world while the world that you live in dissolves beneath your feet, and that your survival depends on completing this construction at least one second before the old habitation collapses.

More than any other work that I have done, this play has seemed to me like the construction of another world, a separate existence. Of course, it is nothing more nor less than my conception of the time and world that I live in, and its people are mostly archetypes of certain basic attitudes and qualities with those mutations that would occur if they had continued along the road to this hypothetical terminal point in it.

A convention of the play is existence outside of time in a place of no specific locality. If you regard it that way, I suppose it becomes an elaborate allegory, but in New Haven we opened directly across the street from a movie theatre that was showing *Peter Pan* in Technicolor and it did not seem altogether inappropriate to me. Fairy tales nearly always have some simple moral lesson of good and evil, but that is not the secret of their fascination any more, I hope, than the philosophical import that might be distilled from the fantasies of *Camino Real* is the principal element of its appeal.

To me the appeal of this work is its unusual degree of freedom. When it began to get under way I felt a new sensation of release, as if I could "ride out" like a tenor sax taking the breaks in a Dixieland combo or a piano in a bop session. You may call it self-indulgence, but I was not doing it merely for

_____

* Written prior to the Broadway premiere of *Camino Real* and published in *The New York Times* on Sunday, March 15, 1953.

myself. I could not have felt a purely private thrill of release unless I had hope of sharing this experience with lots and lots of audiences to come.

My desire was to give these audiences my own sense of something wild and unrestricted that ran like water in the mountains, or clouds changing shape in a gale, or the continually dissolving and transforming images of a dream. This sort of freedom is not chaos nor anarchy. On the contrary, it is the result of painstaking design, and in this work I have given more conscious attention to form and construction than I have in any work before. Freedom is not achieved simply by working freely.

Elia Kazan was attracted to this work mainly, I believe, for the same reason—its freedom and mobility of form. I know that we have kept saying the word "flight" to each other as if the play were merely an abstraction of the impulse to fly, and most of the work out of town, his in staging, mine in cutting and revising, has been with this impulse in mind: the achievement of a continual flow. Speech after speech and bit after bit that were nice in themselves have been remorselessly blasted out of the script and its staging wherever they seemed to obstruct or divert this flow.

There have been plenty of indications already that this play will exasperate and confuse a certain number of people which we hope is not so large as the number it is likely to please. At each performance a number of people have stamped out of the auditorium, with little regard for those whom they have had to crawl over, almost as if the building had caught on fire, and there have been sibilant noises on the way out and demands for money back if the cashier was foolish enough to remain in his box.

I am at a loss to explain this phenomenon, and if I am being facetious about one thing, I am being quite serious about another when I say that I had never for one minute supposed that the play would seem obscure and confusing to anyone who was willing to meet it even less than halfway. It was a costly production, and for this reason I had to read it aloud, together with a few of the actors on one occasion, before large groups of prospective backers, before the funds to produce it were in the till. It was only then that I came up against the disconcerting surprise that some people would think that the play needed clarification.

My attitude is intransigent. I still don't agree that it needs any explanation. Some poet has said that a poem should not mean but be. Of course, a play is not a poem, not even a poetic play has quite the same license as a poem. But to go to *Camino Real* with the inflexible demands of a logician is unfair to both parties.

In Philadelphia a young man from a literary periodical saw the play and then cross-examined me about all its dreamlike images. He had made a list of them while he watched the play, and afterward at my hotel he brought out the list and asked me to explain the meaning of each one. I can't deny that I use a lot of those things called symbols but being a self-defensive creature, I say that symbols are nothing but the natural speech of drama.

We all have in our conscious and unconscious minds a great vocabulary of images, and I think all human communication is based on these images as are our dreams; and a symbol in a play has only one legitimate purpose which is to say a thing more directly and simply and beautifully than it could be said in words.

I hate writing that is a parade of images for the sake of images; I hate it so much that I close a book in disgust when it keeps on saying one thing is like another; I even get disgusted with poems that make nothing but comparisons between one thing and another. But I repeat that symbols, when used respectfully, are the purest language of plays. Sometimes it would take page after tedious page of exposition to put across an idea that can be said with an object or a gesture on the lighted stage.

To take one case in point: the battered portmanteau of Jacques Casanova is hurled from the balcony of a luxury hotel when his remittance check fails to come through. While the portmanteau is still in the air, he shouts: "Careful, I have—" —and when it has crashed to the street he continues—"fragile— mementos . . ." I suppose that is a symbol, at least it is an object used to express as directly and vividly as possible certain things which could be said in pages of dull talk.

As for those patrons who departed before the final scene, I offer myself this tentative bit of solace: that these theatregoers may be a little domesticated in their theatrical tastes. A cage represents security as well as confinement to a bird that has grown used to being in it; and when a theatrical work kicks over the traces with such apparent insouciance, security seems challenged and, instead of participating in its sense of freedom, one out of a certain number of playgoers will rush back out to the more accustomed implausibility of the street he lives on.

To modify this effect of complaisance I would like to admit to you quite frankly that I can't say with any personal conviction that I have written a good play, I only know that I have felt a release in this work which I wanted you to feel with me.

Tennessee Williams

AFTERWORD

Once in a while someone will say to me that he would rather wait for a play to come out as a book than see a live performance of it, where he would be distracted from its true values, if it has any, by so much that is mere spectacle and sensation and consequently must be meretricious and vulgar. There are plays meant for reading. I have read them. I have read the works of "thinking playwrights" as distinguished from us who are permitted only to feel, and probably read them earlier and appreciated them as much as those who invoke their names nowadays like the incantation of Aristophanes' frogs. But the incontinent blaze of a live theatre, a theatre meant for seeing and for feeling, has never been and never will be extinguished by a bucket brigade of critics, new or old, bearing vessels that range from cut-glass punch bowl to Haviland teacup. And in my dissident opinion, a play in a book is only the shadow of a play and not even a clear shadow of it. Those who did not like *Camino Real* on the stage will not be likely to form a higher opinion of it in print, for of all the works I have written, this one was meant most for the vulgarity of performance. The printed script of a play is hardly more than an architect's blueprint of a house not yet built or built and destroyed.

The color, the grace and levitation, the structural pattern in motion, the quick interplay of live beings, suspended like fitful lightning in a cloud, these things are the play, not words on paper, nor thoughts and ideas of an author, those shabby things snatched off basement counters at Gimbel's.

My own creed as a playwright is fairly close to that expressed by the painter in Shaw's play *The Doctor's Dilemma*: "I believe in Michelangelo, Velasquez and Rembrandt; in the might of design, the mystery of color, the redemption of all things by beauty everlasting and the message of art that has made these hands blessed. Amen."

How much art his hands were blessed with or how much mine are, I don't know, but that art is a blessing is certain and that it contains its message is also certain, and I feel, as the painter did, that the message lies in those abstract beauties of form and color and line, to which I would add light and motion.

In these following pages are only the formula by which a play could exist.

Dynamic is a word in disrepute at the moment, and so, I suppose, is the word *organic,* but those terms still define the dramatic values that I value most and which I value more as they are more deprecated by the ones self-appointed to save what they have never known.

Tennessee Williams
June 1, 1953

EDITOR'S NOTE

The version of *Camino Real* here published is considerably revised over the one presented on Broadway. Following the opening there, Mr. Williams went to his home at Key West and continued to work on this play. When he left six weeks later to direct Donald Windham's *The Starless Air* in Houston, Texas, he took the playing version with him and reworked it whenever time allowed. It was with him when he drove in leisurely fashion back to New York. As delivered to the publisher, the manuscript of *Camino Real* was typed on three different typewriters and on stationery of hotels across the country.

Three characters, a prologue and several scenes that were not in the Broadway production have been added, or reinstated from earlier, preproduction versions, while other scenes have been deleted.

Camino Real is divided into a Prologue and Sixteen "Blocks," scenes with no perceptible time lapse between them for the most part. There are intermissions indicated after Block Six and Block Eleven.

The action takes place in an unspecified Latin-American country.

Camino Real was first produced by Cheryl Crawford and Ethel Reiner, in association with Walter P. Chrysler, Jr., and following tryouts in New Haven and Philadelphia, it had its Broadway premiere on March 19, 1953, at the Martin Beck Theatre. The production was directed by Elia Kazan, with the assistance of Anna Sokolow; the setting and costumes were designed by Lemuel Ayers; and incidental music was contributed by Bernardo Ségall. Production associate: Anderson Lawler. Tennessee Williams was represented by Liebling-Wood.

Cast of the Broadway Production

GUTMAN	FRANK SILVERA
SURVIVOR	GUY THOMAJAN
ROSITA	AZA BARD
FIRST OFFICER	HENRY SILVA
JACQUES CASANOVA	JOSEPH ANTHONY
LA MADRECITA DE LOS PERDIDOS	VIVIAN NATHAN
HER SON	ROLANDO VALDEZ
KILROY	ELI WALLACH
FIRST STREETCLEANER	NEHEMIAH PERSOFF
SECOND STREETCLEANER	FRED SADOFF
ABDULLAH	ERNESTO GONZALEZ
A BUM IN A WINDOW	MARTIN BALSAM
A. RATT	MIKE GAZZO
THE LOAN SHARK	SALEM LUDWIG
BARON DE CHARLUS	DAVID J. STEWART
LOBO	RONNE AUL
SECOND OFFICER	WILLIAM LENNARD
A GROTESQUE MUMMER	GLUCK SANDOR
MARGUERITE GAUTIER	JO VAN FLEET

LADY MULLIGAN	LUCILLE PATTON
WAITER	PAGE JOHNSON
LORD BYRON	HURD HATFIELD
NAVIGATOR OF THE FUGITIVO	ANTONY VORNO
PILOT OF THE FUGITIVO	MARTIN BALSAM
MARKET WOMAN	CHARLOTTE JONES
SECOND MARKET WOMAN	JOANNA VISCHER
STREET VENDOR	RUTH VOLNER
LORD MULLIGAN	PARKER WILSON
THE GYPSY	JENNIE GOLDSTEIN
HER DAUGHTER, ESMERALDA	BARBARA BAXLEY
NURSIE	SALEM LUDWIG
EVA	MARY GREY
THE INSTRUCTOR	DAVID J. STEWART
ASSISTANT INSTRUCTOR	PARKER WILSON
MEDICAL STUDENT	PAGE JOHNSON
DON QUIXOTE	HURD HATFIELD
SANCHO PANZA	(*Not in production*)
PRUDENCE DUVERNOY	(*Not in production*)
OLYMPE	(*Not in production*)

Street Vendors: AZA BARD, ERNESTO GONZALEZ, CHARLOTTE JONES, GLUCK SANDOR, JOANNA VISCHER, RUTH VOLNER, ANTONY VORNO.

Guests: MARTIN BALSAM, MARY GREY, LUCILLE PATTON, JOANNA VISCHER, PARKER WILSON.

Passengers: MIKE GAZZO, MARY GREY, PAGE JOHNSON, CHARLOTTE JONES, WILLIAM LENNARD, SALEM LUDWIG, JOANNA VISCHER, RUTH VOLNER.

At the Fiesta: RONNE AUL, MARTIN BALSAM, AZA BARD, MIKE GAZZO, ERNESTO GONZALEZ, MARY GREY, CHARLOTTE JONES, WILLIAM LENNARD, NEHEMIAH PERSOFF, FRED SADOFF, GLUCK SANDOR, JOANNA VISCHER, ANTONY VORNO, PARKER WILSON.

PROLOGUE

As the curtain rises, on an almost lightless stage, there is a loud singing of wind, accompanied by distant, measured reverberations like pounding surf or distant shellfire. Above the ancient wall that backs the set and the perimeter of mountains visible above the wall, are flickers of a white radiance as though daybreak were a white bird caught in a net and struggling to rise.

The plaza is seen fitfully by this light. It belongs to a tropical seaport that bears a confusing, but somehow harmonious, resemblance to such widely scattered ports as Tangiers, Havana, Vera Cruz, Casablanca, Shanghai, New Orleans.

On stage left is the luxury side of the street, containing the façade of the Siete Mares Hotel and its low terrace on which are a number of glass-topped white iron tables and chairs. In the downstairs there is a great bay window in which are seen a pair of elegant "dummies," one seated, one standing behind, looking out into the plaza with painted smiles. Upstairs is a small balcony and behind it a large window exposing a wall on which is hung a phoenix painted on silk: this should be softly lighted now and then in the play, since resurrections are so much a part of its meaning.

Opposite the hotel is Skid Row which contains the Gypsy's gaudy stall, the Loan Shark's establishment with a window containing a variety of pawned articles, and the "Ritz Men Only" which is a flea-bag hotel or flophouse and which has a practical window above its downstairs entrance, in which a bum will appear from time to time to deliver appropriate or contrapuntal song titles.

Upstage is a great flight of stairs that mount the ancient wall to a sort of archway that leads out into "Terra Incognita,"

1

as it is called in the play, a wasteland between the walled town and the distant perimeter of snow-topped mountains.

Downstage right and left are a pair of arches which give entrance to dead-end streets.

Immediately after the curtain rises a shaft of blue light is thrown down a central aisle of the theatre, and in this light, advancing from the back of the house, appears Don Quixote de la Mancha, dressed like an old "desert rat." As he enters the aisle he shouts, "Hola!", in a cracked old voice which is still full of energy and is answered by another voice which is impatient and tired, that of his squire, Sancho Panza. Stumbling with a fatigue which is only physical, the old knight comes down the aisle, and Sancho follows a couple of yards behind him, loaded down with equipment that ranges from a medieval shield to a military canteen or Thermos bottle. Shouts are exchanged between them.

QUIXOTE [*ranting above the wind in a voice which is nearly as old*]:
Blue is the color of distance!

SANCHO [*wearily behind him*]:
Yes, distance is blue.

QUIXOTE:
Blue is also the color of nobility.

SANCHO:
Yes, nobility's blue.

QUIXOTE:
Blue is the color of distance and nobility, and that's why an old knight should always have somewhere about him a bit of blue ribbon . . .

2

[*He jostles the elbow of an aisle-sitter as he staggers with fatigue; he mumbles an apology.*]

SANCHO:
Yes, a bit of blue ribbon.

QUIXOTE:
A bit of faded blue ribbon, tucked away in whatever remains of his armor, or borne on the tip of his lance, his—unconquerable lance! It serves to remind an old knight of distance that he has gone and distance he has yet to go . . .

[*Sancho mutters the Spanish word for excrement as several pieces of rusty armor fall into the aisle.*

[*Quixote has now arrived at the foot of the steps onto the forestage. He pauses there as if wandering out of or into a dream. Sancho draws up clanking behind him.*

[*Mr. Gutman, a lordly fat man wearing a linen suit and a pith helmet, appears dimly on the balcony of the Siete Mares, a white cockatoo on his wrist. The bird cries out harshly.*]

GUTMAN:
Hush, Aurora.

QUIXOTE:
It also reminds an old knight of that green country he lived in which was the youth of his heart, before such singing words as *Truth!*

SANCHO [*panting*]:
—Truth.

QUIXOTE:
Valor!

3

SANCHO:
—Valor.

QUIXOTE [*elevating his lance*]:
Devoir!

SANCHO:
—Devoir ...

QUIXOTE:
—turned into the meaningless mumble of some old monk hunched over cold mutton at supper!

[*Gutman alerts a pair of Guards in the plaza, who cross with red lanterns to either side of the proscenium where they lower black and white striped barrier gates as if the proscenium marked a frontier. One of them, with a hand on his holster, advances toward the pair on the steps.*]

GUARD:
Vien aquí.

[*Sancho hangs back but Quixote stalks up to the barrier gate. The Guard turns a flashlight on his long and exceedingly grave red face, "frisks" him casually for concealed weapons, examines a rusty old knife and tosses it contemptuously away.*]

Sus papeles! Sus documentos!

[*Quixote fumblingly produces some tattered old papers from the lining of his hat.*]

GUTMAN [*impatiently*]:
Who is it?

GUARD:
An old desert rat named Quixote.

GUTMAN:

Oh!—Expected!—Let him in.

[*The Guards raise the barrier gate and one sits down to smoke on the terrace. Sancho hangs back still. A dispute takes place on the forestage and steps into the aisle.*]

QUIXOTE:

Forward!

SANCHO:

Aw, naw. I know this place. [*He produces a crumpled parchment.*] Here it is on the chart. Look, it says here: "Continue until you come to the square of a walled town which is the end of the *Camino Real* and the beginning of the *Camino Real*. Halt there," it says, "and turn back, Traveler, for the spring of humanity has gone dry in this place and—"

QUIXOTE [*He snatches the chart from him and reads the rest of the inscription.*]:

"—there are no birds in the country except wild birds that are tamed and kept in—" [*He holds the chart close to his nose.*]

—Cages!

SANCHO [*urgently*]:

Let's go back to La Mancha!

QUIXOTE:

Forward!

SANCHO:

The time has come for retreat!

QUIXOTE:

The time for retreat never comes!

SANCHO:
I'm going back to *La Mancha!*
[*He dumps the knightly equipment into the orchestra pit.*]

QUIXOTE:
Without me?

SANCHO [*bustling up the aisle*]:
With you or without you, old tireless and tiresome master!

QUIXOTE [*imploringly*]:
Saaaaaan-choooooooooo!

SANCHO [*near the top of the aisle*]:
I'm going back to La *Maaaaaaaaan-chaaaaaaa* . . .

[*He disappears as the blue light in the aisle dims out. The Guard puts out his cigarette and wanders out of the plaza. The wind moans and Gutman laughs softly as the Ancient Knight enters the plaza with such a desolate air.*]

QUIXOTE [*looking about the plaza*]:
—Lonely . . .

[*To his surprise the word is echoed softly by almost unseen figures huddled below the stairs and against the wall of the town. Quixote leans upon his lance and observes with a wry smile—*]

—When so many are lonely as seem to be lonely, it would be inexcusably selfish to be lonely alone.

[*He shakes out a dusty blanket. Shadowy arms extend toward him and voices murmur.*]

VOICE:
Sleep. Sleep. Sleep.

6

QUIXOTE [*arranging his blanket*]:
Yes, I'll sleep for a while, I'll sleep and dream for a while against the wall of this town . . .

[*A mandolin or guitar plays "The Nightingale of France."*]

—And my dream will be a pageant, a masque in which old meanings will be remembered and possibly new ones discovered, and when I wake from this sleep and this disturbing pageant of a dream, I'll choose one among its shadows to take along with me in the place of Sancho . . .

[*He blows his nose between his fingers and wipes them on his shirttail.*]

—For new companions are not as familiar as old ones but all the same—they're old ones with only slight differences of face and figure, which may or may not be improvements, and it would be selfish of me to be lonely alone . . .

[*He stumbles down the incline into the Pit below the stairs where most of the Street People huddle beneath awnings of open stalls.*]

[*The white cockatoo squawks.*]

GUTMAN:
Hush, Aurora.

QUIXOTE:
And tomorrow at this same hour, which we call madrugada, the loveliest of all words, except the word alba, and that word also means daybreak—
—Yes, at daybreak tomorrow I will go on from here with a new companion and this old bit of blue ribbon to keep me in mind of distance that I have gone and distance I have yet to go, and also to keep me in mind of—

[*The cockatoo cries wildly.*

[*Quixote nods as if in agreement with the outcry and folds himself into his blanket below the great stairs.*]

GUTMAN [*stroking the cockatoo's crest*]:
Be still, Aurora. I know it's morning, Aurora.

[*Daylight turns the plaza silver and slowly gold. Vendors rise beneath white awnings of stalls. The Gypsy's stall opens. A tall, courtly figure, in his late middle years (Jacques Casanova) crosses from the Siete Mares to the Loan Shark's, removing a silver snuffbox from his pocket as Gutman speaks. His costume, like that of all the legendary characters in the play (except perhaps Quixote) is generally "modern" but with vestigial touches of the period to which he was actually related. The cane and the snuffbox and perhaps a brocaded vest may be sufficient to give this historical suggestion in Casanova's case. He bears his hawklike head with a sort of anxious pride on most occasions, a pride maintained under a steadily mounting pressure.*]

—It's morning and after morning. It's afternoon, ha ha! And now I must go downstairs to announce the beginning of that old wanderer's dream ...

[*He withdraws from the balcony as old Prudence Duvernoy stumbles out of the hotel, as if not yet quite awake from an afternoon siesta. Chattering with beads and bracelets, she wanders vaguely down into the plaza, raising a faded green silk parasol, damp henna-streaked hair slipping under a monstrous hat of faded silk roses; she is searching for a lost poodle.*]

PRUDENCE:
Trique? Trique?

[*Jacques comes out of the Loan Shark's replacing his case angrily in his pocket.*]

JACQUES:

Why, I'd rather give it to a street beggar! This case is a Boucheron, I won it at faro at the summer palace, at Tsarskoe Selo in the winter of—

[*The Loan Shark slams the door. Jacques glares, then shrugs and starts across the plaza. Old Prudence is crouched over the filthy gray bundle of a dying mongrel by the fountain.*]

PRUDENCE:

Trique, oh, Trique!

[*The Gypsy's son, Abdullah, watches, giggling.*]

JACQUES [*reproving*]:

It is a terrible thing for an old woman to outlive her dogs.

[*He crosses to Prudence and gently disengages the animal from her grasp.*]

Madam, that is not Trique.

PRUDENCE:

—When I woke up she wasn't in her basket . . .

JACQUES:

Sometimes we sleep too long in the afternoon and when we wake we find things changed, Signora.

PRUDENCE:

Oh, you're Italian!

JACQUES:

I am from Venice, Signora.

PRUDENCE:

Ah, Venice, city of pearls! I saw you last night on the terrace

9

dining with—Oh, I'm so worried about her! I'm an old friend of hers, perhaps she's mentioned me to you. Prudence Duvernoy? I was her best friend in the old days in Paris, but now she's forgotten so much . . .

I hope you have influence with her!

[*A waltz of Camille's time in Paris is heard.*]

I want you to give her a message from a certain wealthy old gentleman that she met at one of those watering places she used to go to for her health. She resembled his daughter who died of consumption and so he adored Camille, lavished everything on her! What did she do? Took a young lover who hadn't a couple of pennies to rub together, disinherited by his father because of *her!* Oh, you can't do that, not now, not any more, you've got to be realistic on the Camino Real!

[*Gutman has come out on the terrace: he announces quietly—*]

GUTMAN:
Block One on the Camino Real.

PRUDENCE [*continuing*]:

Yes, you've got to be practical on it! Well, give her this message, please, Sir. He wants her back on any terms whatsoever! [*Her speech gathers furious momentum.*] Her evenings will be free. He wants only her mornings, mornings are hard on old men because their hearts beat slowly, and he wants only her mornings! Well, that's how it should be! A sensible arrangement! Elderly gentlemen have to content themselves with a lady's spare time before supper! Isn't that so? Of course so! And so I told him! I told him, Camille isn't well! She requires delicate care! Has many debts, creditors storm her door! "How much does she owe?" he asked me, and, oh, did I do some lightning mathematics! Jewels in pawn, I told him, pearls, rings, necklaces, bracelets, diamond eardrops are in pawn! Horses put up for sale at a public auction!

JACQUES [*appalled by this torrent*]:
Signora, Signora, all of these things are—

PRUDENCE:
—What?

JACQUES:
Dreams!

[*Gutman laughs. A woman sings at a distance.*]

PRUDENCE [*continuing with less assurance*]:
—You're not so young as I thought when I saw you last night on the terrace by candlelight on the—Oh, but—Ho ho!—I bet there is *one* old fountain in this plaza that hasn't gone dry!

[*She pokes him obscenely. He recoils. Gutman laughs. Jacques starts away but she seizes his arm again, and the torrent of speech continues.*]

11

PRUDENCE:

Wait, wait, listen! Her candle is burning low. But how can you tell? She might have a lingering end, and charity hospitals? Why, you might as well take a flying leap into the Streetcleaners' barrel. Oh, I've told her and told her not to live in a dream! A dream is nothing to live in, why, it's gone like a—

Don't let her elegance fool you! That girl has done the Camino in carriages but she has also done it on foot! She knows every stone the Camino is paved with! So tell her this. You tell her, she won't listen to me!—Times and conditions have undergone certain changes since we were friends in Paris, and now we dismiss young lovers with skins of silk and eyes like a child's first prayer, we put them away as lightly as we put away white gloves meant only for summer, and pick up a pair of black ones, suitable for winter . . .

[*The singing voice rises: then subsides.*]

JACQUES:

Excuse me, Madam.

[*He tears himself from her grasp and rushes into the Siete Mares.*]

PRUDENCE [*dazed, to Gutman*]:

—What block is this?

GUTMAN:

Block One.

PRUDENCE:

I didn't hear the announcement . . .

GUTMAN [*coldly*]:

Well, now you do.

12

[*Olympe comes out of the lobby with a pale orange silk parasol like a floating moon.*]

OLYMPE:

Oh, there you are, I've looked for you high and low!—mostly low ...

[*They float vaguely out into the dazzling plaza as though a capricious wind took them, finally drifting through the Moorish arch downstage right.*

[*The song dies out.*]

GUTMAN [*lighting a thin cigar*]:

Block Two on the Camino Real.

BLOCK TWO

After Gutman's announcement, a hoarse cry is heard. A figure in rags, skin blackened by the sun, tumbles crazily down the steep alley to the plaza. He turns about blindly, murmuring: "A donde la fuente?" He stumbles against the hideous old prostitute Rosita who grins horribly and whispers something to him, hitching up her ragged, filthy skirt. Then she gives him a jocular push toward the fountain. He falls upon his belly and thrusts his hands into the dried-up basin. Then he staggers to his feet with a despairing cry.

THE SURVIVOR:
La fuente está seca!

[*Rosita laughs madly but the other Street People moan. A dry gourd rattles.*]

ROSITA:
The fountain is dry, but there's plenty to drink in the Siete Mares!

[*She shoves him toward the hotel. The proprietor, Gutman, steps out, smoking a thin cigar, fanning himself with a palm leaf. As the Survivor advances, Gutman whistles. A man in military dress comes out upon the low terrace.*]

OFFICER:
Go back!

[*The Survivor stumbles forward. The Officer fires at him. He lowers his hands to his stomach, turns slowly about with a lost expression, looking up at the sky, and stumbles toward the fountain. During the scene that follows, until the entrance of La Madrecita and her Son, the Survivor drags*

14

*himself slowly about the concrete rim of the fountain,
almost entirely ignored, as a dying pariah dog in a starving
country. Jacques Casanova comes out upon the terrace of
the Siete Mares. Now he passes the hotel proprietor's im-
passive figure, descending a step beneath and a little in
advance of him, and without looking at him.*]

JACQUES [*with infinite weariness and disgust*]:
What has happened?

GUTMAN [*serenely*]:

We have entered the second in a progress of sixteen blocks on
the Camino Real. It's five o'clock. That angry old lion, the
Sun, looked back once and growled and then went switching
his tail toward the cool shade of the Sierras. Our guests have
taken their afternoon siestas . . .

[*The Survivor has come out upon the forestage, now, not
like a dying man but like a shy speaker who has forgotten
the opening line of his speech. He is only a little crouched
over with a hand obscuring the red stain over his belly. Two
or three Street People wander about calling their wares:
"Tacos, tacos, fritos . . ."—"Lotería, lotería"—Rosita shuffles
around, calling "Love? Love?"—pulling down the filthy
décolletage of her blouse to show more of her sagging
bosom. The Survivor arrives at the top of the stairs descending into the orchestra of the theatre, and hangs onto it,
looking out reflectively as a man over the rail of a boat
coming into a somewhat disturbingly strange harbor.*]

GUTMAN [*continuing*]:
—They suffer from extreme fatigue, our guests at the Siete
Mares, all of them have a degree or two of fever. Questions
are passed amongst them like something illicit and shameful,
like counterfeit money or drugs or indecent post cards—

15

[*He leans forward and whispers:*]

—"What is this place? Where are we? What is the meaning of—*Shhhh!*"—Ha ha . . .

THE SURVIVOR [*very softly to the audience*]:
I once had a pony named Peeto. He caught in his nostrils the scent of thunderstorms coming even before the clouds had crossed the Sierra . . .

VENDOR:
Tacos, tacos, fritos . . .

ROSITA:
Love? Love?

LADY MULLIGAN [*to waiter on terrace*]:
Are you sure no one called me? I was expecting a call . . .

GUTMAN [*smiling*]:
My guests are confused and exhausted but at this hour they pull themselves together, and drift downstairs on the wings of gin and the lift, they drift into the public rooms and exchange notes again on fashionable couturiers and custom tailors, restaurants, vintages of wine, hairdressers, plastic surgeons, girls and young men susceptible to offers . . .

[*There is a hum of light conversation and laughter within.*]

—Hear them? They're exchanging notes . . .

JACQUES [*striking the terrace with his cane*]:
I asked you what has happened in the plaza!

GUTMAN:
Oh, in the plaza, ha ha!—Happenings in the plaza don't concern us . . .

16

JACQUES:
I heard shots fired.

GUTMAN:
Shots were fired to remind you of your good fortune in staying here. The public fountains have gone dry, you know, but the Siete Mares was erected over the only perpetual never-dried-up spring in Tierra Caliente, and of course that advantage has to be—protected—sometimes by—martial law . . .

[*The guitar resumes.*]

THE SURVIVOR:
When Peeto, my pony, was born—he stood on his four legs at once, and accepted the world!—He was wiser than I . . .

VENDOR:
Fritos, fritos, tacos!

ROSITA:
Love!

THE SURVIVOR:
—When Peeto was one year old he was wiser than God!

[*A wind sings across the plaza; a dry gourd rattles.*]

"Peeto, Peeto!" the Indian boys call after him, trying to stop him—trying to stop the wind!

[*The Survivor's head sags forward. He sits down as slowly as an old man on a park bench. Jacques strikes the terrace again with his cane and starts toward the Survivor. The Guard seizes his elbow.*]

JACQUES:
Don't put your hand on *me*!

GUARD:
Stay here.

GUTMAN:
Remain on the terrace, please, Signor Casanova.

JACQUES [*fiercely*]:
—*Cognac!*

[*The Waiter whispers to Gutman. Gutman chuckles.*]

GUTMAN:
The Maître 'D' tells me that your credit has been discontinued
in the restaurant and bar, he says that he has enough of your
tabs to pave the terrace with!

JACQUES:
What a piece of impertinence! I told the man that the letter
that I'm expecting has been delayed in the mail. The postal
service in this country is fantastically disorganized, and you
know it! You also know that Mlle. Gautier will guarantee my
tabs!

GUTMAN:
Then let her pick them up at dinner tonight if you're hungry!

JACQUES:
I'm not accustomed to this kind of treatment on the Camino
Real!

GUTMAN:
Oh, you'll be, you'll be, after a single night at the "Ritz Men
Only." That's where you'll have to transfer your patronage if
the letter containing the remittance check doesn't arrive tonight.

JACQUES:

I assure you that I shall do nothing of the sort!—Tonight or ever!

GUTMAN:

Watch out, old hawk, the wind is ruffling your feathers!

[*Jacques sinks trembling into a chair.*]

—Give him a thimble of brandy before he collapses . . . Fury is a luxury of the young, their veins are resilient, but his are brittle . . .

JACQUES:

Here I sit, submitting to insult for a thimble of brandy— while directly in front of me—

[*The singer, La Madrecita, enters the plaza. She is a blind woman led by a ragged Young Man. The Waiter brings Jacques a brandy.*]

—a man in the plaza dies like a pariah dog!—I take the brandy! I sip it!—My heart is too tired to break, my heart is too tired to—break . . .

[*La Madrecita chants softly. She slowly raises her arm to point at the Survivor crouched on the steps from the plaza.*]

GUTMAN [*suddenly*]:

Give me the phone! Connect me with the Palace. Get me the Generalissimo, quick, quick, quick!

[*The Survivor rises feebly and shuffles very slowly toward the extended arms of "The Little Blind One."*]

Generalissimo? Gutman speaking! Hello, sweetheart. There has been a little incident in the plaza. You know that party of

19

young explorers that attempted to cross the desert on foot? Well, one of them's come back. He was very thirsty. He found the fountain dry. He started toward the hotel. He was politely advised to advance no further. But he disregarded this advice. Action had to be taken. And now, and now—that old blind woman they call "La Madrecita"?—She's come into the plaza with the man called "The Dreamer" . . .

SURVIVOR:
Donde?

THE DREAMER:
Aquí!

GUTMAN [*continuing*]:
You remember those two! I once mentioned them to you. You said "They're harmless dreamers and they're loved by the people."—"What," I asked you, "is harmless about a dreamer, and what," I asked you, "is harmless about the love of the people?—Revolution only needs good dreamers who remember their dreams, and the love of the people belongs safely only to you—their Generalissimo!"—Yes, now the blind woman has recovered her sight and is extending her arms to the wounded Survivor, and the man with the guitar is leading him to her . . .

[*The described action is being enacted.*]

Wait one moment! There's a possibility that the forbidden word may be spoken! Yes! The forbidden word is about to be spoken!

[*The Dreamer places an arm about the blinded Survivor, and cries out:*]

THE DREAMER:
Hermano!

[*The cry is repeated like springing fire and a loud murmur sweeps the crowd. They push forward with cupped hands extended and the gasping cries of starving people at the sight of bread. Two Military Guards herd them back under the colonnades with clubs and drawn revolvers. La Madrecita chants softly with her blind eyes lifted. A Guard starts toward her. The People shout "NO!"*]

LA MADRECITA [*chanting*]:
"Rojo está el sol! Rojo está el sol de sangre! Blanca está la luna! Blanca está la luna de miedo!"

[*The crowd makes a turning motion.*]

GUTMAN [*to the waiter*]:
Put up the ropes!

[*Velvet ropes are strung very quickly about the terrace of the Siete Mares. They are like the ropes on decks of steamers in rough waters. Gutman shouts into the phone again:*]

The word was spoken. The crowd is agitated. Hang on!

[*He lays down instrument.*]

JACQUES [*hoarsely, shaken*]:
He said "Hermano." That's the word for brother.

GUTMAN [*calmly*]:
Yes, the most dangerous word in any human tongue is the word for brother. It's inflammatory.—I don't suppose it can be struck out of the language altogether but it must be reserved for strictly private usage in back of soundproof walls. Otherwise it disturbs the population . . .

JACQUES:
The people need the word. They're thirsty for it!

GUTMAN:

What are these creatures? Mendicants. Prostitutes. Thieves and petty vendors in a bazaar where the human heart is a part of the bargain.

JACQUES:

Because they need the word and the word is forbidden!

GUTMAN:

The word is said in pulpits and at tables of council where its volatile essence can be contained. But on the lips of these creatures, what is it? A wanton incitement to riot, without understanding. For what is a brother to them but someone to get ahead of, to cheat, to lie to, to undersell in the market. Brother, you say to a man whose wife you sleep with!—But now, you see, the word has disturbed the people and made it necessary to invoke martial law!

[*Meanwhile the Dreamer has brought the Survivor to La Madrecita, who is seated on the cement rim of the fountain. She has cradled the dying man in her arms in the attitude of a* Pietà. *The Dreamer is crouched beside them, softly playing a guitar. Now he springs up with a harsh cry:*]

THE DREAMER:

Muerto!

[*The Streetcleaners' piping commences at a distance. Gutman seizes the phone again.*]

GUTMAN [*into phone*]:

Generalissimo, the Survivor is no longer surviving. I think we'd better have some public diversion right away. Put the Gypsy on! Have her announce the Fiesta!

LOUDSPEAKER [*responding instantly*]:
Damas y Caballeros! The next voice you hear will be the
voice of—the Gypsy!

GYPSY [*over loudspeaker*]:
Hoy! Noche de Fiesta! Tonight the moon will restore the
virginity of my daughter!

GUTMAN:
Bring on the Gypsy's daughter, Esmeralda. Show the virgin-
to-be!

[*Esmeralda is led from the Gypsy's stall by a severe duenna,
"Nursie," out upon the forestage. She is manacled by the
wrist to the duenna. Her costume is vaguely Levantine.*]

[*Guards are herding the crowd back again.*]

GUTMAN:
Ha ha! Ho ho ho! Music!

[*There is gay music. Rosita dances.*]

Abdullah! You're on!

[*Abdullah skips into the plaza, shouting histrionically.*]

ABDULLAH:
Tonight the moon will restore the virginity of my sister,
Esmeralda!

GUTMAN:
Dance, boy!

[*Esmeralda is led back into the stall. Throwing off his
burnoose, Abdullah dances with Rosita. Behind their dance,
armed Guards force La Madrecita and the Dreamer to
retreat from the fountain, leaving the lifeless body of the*

23

Survivor. All at once there is a discordant blast of brass instruments.

[Kilroy comes into the plaza. He is a young American vagrant, about twenty-seven. He wears dungarees and a skivvy shirt, the pants faded nearly white from long wear and much washing, fitting him as closely as the clothes of sculpture. He has a pair of golden boxing gloves slung about his neck and he carries a small duffle bag. His belt is ruby-and-emerald-studded with the word CHAMP in bold letters. He stops before a chalked inscription on a wall downstage which says: "Kilroy Is Coming!" He scratches out "Coming" and over it prints "Here!"]

GUTMAN:

Ho ho!—a clown! The Eternal Punchinella! That's exactly what's needed in a time of crisis!

Block Three on the Camino Real.

BLOCK THREE

KILROY [*genially, to all present*]:
Ha ha!

[*Then he walks up to the Officer by the terrace of the Siete Mares.*]

Buenas dias, señor.

[*He gets no response—barely even a glance.*]

Habla Inglesia? Usted?

OFFICER:
What is it you want?

KILROY:
Where is Western Union or Wells-Fargo? I got to send a wire to some friends in the States.

OFFICER:
No hay Western Union, no hay Wells-Fargo.

KILROY:
That is very peculiar. I never struck a town yet that didn't have one or the other. I just got off a boat. Lousiest frigging tub I ever shipped on, one continual hell it was, all the way up from Rio. And me sick, too. I picked up one of those tropical fevers. No sick bay on that tub, no doctor, no medicine or nothing, not even one quinine pill, and I was burning up with Christ knows how much fever. I couldn't make them understand I was sick. I got a bad heart, too. I had to retire from the prize ring because of my heart. I was the light heavyweight champion of the West Coast, won these gloves! —before my ticker went bad.—Feel my chest! Go on, feel it! Feel it. I've got a heart in my chest as big as the head of a baby. Ha ha! They stood me in front of a screen that makes

you transparent and that's what they seen inside me, a heart in my chest as big as the head of a baby! With something like that you don't need the Gypsy to tell you, "Time is short, Baby —get ready to hitch on wings!" The medics wouldn't okay me for no more fights. They said to give up liquor and smoking and sex!—To give up sex!—I used to believe a man couldn't live without sex—but he can—if he wants to! My real true woman, my wife, she would of stuck with me, but it was all spoiled with her being scared and me, too, that a real hard kiss would kill me!—So one night while she was sleeping I wrote her good-bye . . .

[*He notices a lack of attention in the Officer: he grins.*]

No comprendo the lingo?

OFFICER:
What is it you want?

KILROY:
Excuse my ignorance, but what place is this? What is this country and what is the name of this town? I know it seems funny of me to ask such a question. Loco! But I was so glad to get off that rotten tub that I didn't ask nothing of no one except my pay—and I got shortchanged on that. I have trouble counting these pesos or Whatzit-you-call-'em.

[*He jerks out his wallet.*]

All-a-this-here. In the States that pile of lettuce would make you a plutocrat!—But I bet you this stuff don't add up to fifty dollars American coin. Ha ha!

OFFICER:
Ha ha.

26

KILROY:

Ha ha!

OFFICER [*making it sound like a death rattle*]:
Ha-ha-ha-ha-ha.

[*He turns and starts into the cantina. Kilroy grabs his arm.*]

KILROY:

Hey!

OFFICER:

What is it you want?

KILROY:

What is the name of this country and this town?

[*The Officer thrusts his elbow in Kilroy's stomach and twists his arm loose with a Spanish curse. He kicks the swinging doors open and enters the cantina.*]

Brass hats are the same everywhere.

[*As soon as the Officer goes, the Street People come forward and crowd about Kilroy with their wheedling cries.*]

STREET PEOPLE:

Dulces, dulces! Lotería! Lotería! Pasteles, café con leche!

KILROY:

No caree, no caree!

[*The Prostitute creeps up to him and grins.*]

ROSITA:

Love? Love?

KILROY:

What did you say?

27

ROSITA:

Love?

KILROY:

Sorry—I don't feature that. [*to audience*] I have ideals.

[*The Gypsy appears on the roof of her establishment with Esmeralda whom she secures by handcuffs to the iron railing.*]

GYPSY:

Stay there while I give the pitch!

[*She then advances with a portable microphone.*]

Testing! One, two, three, four!

NURSIE [*from offstage*]:

You're on the air!

GYPSY'S LOUDSPEAKER:

Are you perplexed by something? Are you tired out and confused? Do you have a fever?

[*Kilroy looks around for the source of the voice.*]

Do you feel yourself to be spiritually unprepared for the age of exploding atoms? Do you distrust the newspapers? Are you suspicious of governments? Have you arrived at a point on the Camino Real where the walls converge not in the distance but right in front of your nose? Does further progress appear impossible to you? Are you afraid of anything at all? Afraid of your heartbeat? Or the eyes of strangers! Afraid of breathing? Afraid of not breathing? Do you wish that things could be straight and simple again as they were in your childhood? Would you like to go back to Kindy Garten?

[*Rosita has crept up to Kilroy while he listens. She reaches out to him. At the same time a Pickpocket lifts his wallet.*]

KILROY [*catching the whore's wrist*]:
Keep y'r hands off me, y' dirty ole bag! No caree putas! No loteria, no dulces, nada—so get away! Vamoose! All of you! Quit picking at me!

[*He reaches in his pocket and jerks out a handful of small copper and silver coins which he flings disgustedly down the street. The grotesque people scramble after it with their inhuman cries. Kilroy goes on a few steps—then stops short —feeling the back pocket of his dungarees. Then he lets out a startled cry.*]

Robbed! My God, I've been robbed!

[*The Street People scatter to the walls.*]

Which of you got my wallet? *Which* of you dirty—? Shh–Uh!

[*They mumble with gestures of incomprehension. He marches back to the entrance to the hotel.*]

Hey! Officer! Official!—General!

[*The Officer finally lounges out of the hotel entrance and glances at Kilroy.*]

Tiende? One of them's got my wallet! Picked it out of my pocket while that old whore there was groping me! Don't you comprendo?

OFFICER:
Nobody rob you. You don't have no pesos.

KILROY:
Huh?

29

OFFICER:

You just dreaming that you have money. You don't ever have money. Nunca! Nada!

[*He spits between his teeth.*]

Loco . . .

[*The Officer crosses to the fountain. Kilroy stares at him, then bawls out:*]

KILROY [*to the Street People*]:

We'll see what the American Embassy has to say about this! I'll go to the American Consul. Whichever of you rotten spivs lifted my wallet is going to jail—calaboose! I hope I have made myself plain. If not, I will make myself plainer!

[*There are scattered laughs among the crowd. He crosses to the fountain. He notices the body of the no longer Survivor, kneels beside it, shakes it, turns it over, springs up and shouts:*]

Hey! This guy is dead!

[*There is the sound of the Streetcleaners' piping. They trundle their white barrel into the plaza from one of the downstage arches. The appearance of these men undergoes a progressive alteration through the play. When they first appear they are almost like any such public servants in a tropical country; their white jackets are dirtier than the musicians' and some of the stains are red. They have on white caps with black visors. They are continually exchanging sly jokes and giggling unpleasantly together. Lord Mulligan has come out upon the terrace and as they pass him, they pause for a moment, point at him, snicker. He is extremely discomfited by this impertinence, touches his chest as if he felt a palpitation and turns back inside.*]

[*Kilroy yells to the advancing Streetcleaners.*]

There's a dead man layin' here!

[*They giggle again. Briskly they lift the body and stuff it into the barrel; then trundle it off, looking back at Kilroy, giggling, whispering. They return under the downstage arch through which they entered. Kilroy, in a low, shocked voice:*]

What *is* this place? What kind of a hassle have I got myself into?

LOUDSPEAKER:

If anyone on the Camino is bewildered, come to the Gypsy. A poco dinero will tickle the Gypsy's palm and give her visions!

ABDULLAH [*giving Kilroy a card*]:

If you got a question, ask my mama, the Gypsy!

KILROY:

Man, whenever you see those three brass balls on a street, you don't have to look a long ways for a Gypsy. Now le' me think. I am faced with three problems. One: I'm hungry. Two: I'm lonely. Three: I'm in a place where I don't know what it is or how I got there! First action that's indicated is to—cash in on something—Well . . . let's see . . .

[*Honky-tonk music fades in at this point and the Skid Row façade begins to light up for the evening. There is the Gypsy's stall with its cabalistic devices, its sectional cranium and palm, three luminous brass balls overhanging the entrance to the Loan Shark and his window filled with a vast assortment of hocked articles for sale: trumpets, banjos, fur coats, tuxedos, a gown of scarlet sequins, loops of pearls and rhinestones. Dimly behind this display is a neon sign*] *in three pastel colors, pink, green, and blue. It fades softly in and out and it says: "Magic Tricks Jokes." There is also the advertisement of a flea-bag hotel or flophouse called "Ritz Men Only." This sign is also pale neon or luminous paint, and only the entrance is on the street floor, the rooms are above the Loan Shark and Gypsy's stall. One of the windows of this upper story is practical. Figures appear in it sometimes, leaning out as if suffocating or to hawk and spit into the street below. This side of the street should have all the color and animation that are permitted by the resources of the production. There may be moments of dancelike action (a fight, a seduction, sale of narcotics, arrest, etc.).]*

KILROY [*to the audience from the apron*]:
What've I got to cash in on? My golden gloves? Never! I'll say that once more, never! The silver-framed photo of my One True Woman? Never! Repeat that! Never! What else have I got of a detachable and a negotiable nature? Oh! My ruby-and-emerald-studded belt with the word CHAMP on it.

[*He whips it off his pants.*]

This is not necessary to hold on my pants, but this is a precious reminder of the sweet used-to-be. Oh, well. Sometimes a man has got to hock his sweet used-to-be in order to finance his present situation . . .

[*He enters the Loan Shark's. A Drunken Bum leans out the practical window of the "Ritz Men Only" and shouts:*]

BUM:

O Jack o' Diamonds, you robbed my pockets, you robbed my pockets of silver and gold!

[*He jerks the window shade down.*]

GUTMAN [*on the terrace*]:

Block Four on the Camino Real!

BLOCK FOUR

There is a phrase of light music as the Baron de Charlus, an elderly foppish sybarite in a light silk suit, a carnation in his lapel, crosses from the Siete Mares to the honky-tonk side of the street. On his trail is a wild-looking young man of startling beauty called Lobo. Charlus is aware of the follower and, during his conversation with A. Ratt, he takes out a pocket mirror to inspect him while pretending to comb his hair and point his moustache. As Charlus approaches, the Manager of the flea-bag puts up a vacancy sign and calls out:

A. RATT:

Vacancy here! A bed at the "Ritz Men Only"! A little white ship to sail the dangerous night in . . .

THE BARON:

Ah, bon soir, Mr. Ratt.

A. RATT:

Cruising?

THE BARON:

No, just—walking!

A. RATT:

That's all you need to do.

THE BARON:

I sometimes find it suffices. You have a vacancy, do you?

A. RATT:

For you?

THE BARON:

And a possible guest. You know the requirements. An iron bed with no mattress and a considerable length of stout knotted rope. No! Chains this evening, metal chains. I've been very bad, I have a lot to atone for . . .

A. RATT:

Why don't you take these joy rides at the Siete Mares?

THE BARON [*with the mirror focused on Lobo*]:

They don't have Ingreso Libero at the Siete Mares. Oh, I don't like places in the haute saison, the alta staggione, and yet if you go between the fashionable seasons, it's too hot or too damp or appallingly overrun by all the wrong sort of people who rap on the wall if canaries sing in your bedsprings after midnight. I don't know why such people don't stay at home. Surely a Kodak, a Brownie, or even a Leica works just as well in Milwaukee or Sioux City as it does in these places they do on their whirlwind summer tours, and don't look now, but I think I am being followed!

A. RATT:

Yep, you've made a pickup!

THE BARON:

Attractive?

A. RATT:

That depends on who's driving the bicycle, Dad.

THE BARON:

Ciao, Caro! Expect me at ten.

[*He crosses elegantly to the fountain.*]

A. RATT:

Vacancy here! A little white ship to sail the dangerous night in!

[*The music changes. Kilroy backs out of the Loan Shark's, belt unsold, engaged in a violent dispute. The Loan Shark is haggling for his golden gloves. Charlus lingers, intrigued by the scene.*]

LOAN SHARK:

I don't want no belt! I want the gloves! Eight-fifty!

KILROY:

No dice.

LOAN SHARK:

Nine, nine-fifty!

KILROY:

Nah, nah, nah!

LOAN SHARK:

Yah, yah, yah.

KILROY:

I say nah.

LOAN SHARK:

I say yah.

KILROY:

The nahs have it.

LOAN SHARK:

Don't be a fool. What can you do with a pair of golden gloves?

KILROY:

I can remember the battles I fought to win them! I can remember that I used to be—CHAMP!

[*Fade in Band Music: "March of the Gladiators"—ghostly cheers, etc.*]

LOAN SHARK:

You can remember that you *used to be*—Champ?

KILROY:

Yes! I used to be—CHAMP!

THE BARON:

Used to be is the past tense, meaning useless.

KILROY:

Not to me, Mister. These are my gloves, these gloves are gold, and I fought a lot of hard fights to win 'em! I broke clean from the clinches. I never hit a low blow, the referee never told me to mix it up! And the fixers never got to me!

LOAN SHARK:

In other words, a sucker!

KILROY:

Yep, I'm a sucker that won the golden gloves!

LOAN SHARK:

Congratulations. My final offer is a piece of green paper with Alexander Hamilton's picture on it. Take it or leave it.

KILROY:

I leave it for you to *stuff* it! I'd hustle my heart on this street, I'd peddle my heart's true blood before I'd leave my golden gloves hung up in a loan shark's window between a rusted trombone and some poor lush's long-ago mildewed tuxedo!

LOAN SHARK:

So you say but I will see you later.

THE BARON:

The name of the Camino is not unreal!

[*The Bum sticks his head out the window and shouts:*]

BUM:

Pa dam, Pa dam, Pa dam!

THE BARON [*continuing the Bum's song*]:
Echoes the beat of my heart!
Pa dam, Pa dam—*hello!*

[*He has crossed to Kilroy as he sings and extends his hand
to him.*]

KILROY [*uncertainly*]:
Hey, mate. It's wonderful to see you.

THE BARON:
Thanks, but why?

KILROY:
A normal American. In a clean white suit.

THE BARON:
My suit is pale yellow. My nationality is French, and my
normality has been often subject to question.

KILROY:
I still say your suit is clean.

THE BARON:
Thanks. That's more than I can say for your apparel.

KILROY:
Don't judge a book by the covers. I'd take a shower if I could
locate the "Y."

THE BARON:
What's the "Y"?

KILROY:
Sort of a Protestant church with a swimmin' pool in it. Some-

times it also has an employment bureau. It does good in the community.

THE BARON:
Nothing in this community does much good.

KILROY:
I'm getting the same impression. This place is confusing to me. I think it must be the aftereffects of fever. Nothing seems real. Could you give me the scoop?

THE BARON:
Serious questions are referred to the Gypsy. Once upon a time. Oh, once upon a time. I used to wonder. Now I simply wander. I stroll about the fountain and hope to be followed. Some people call it corruption. I call it—simplification . . .

BUM [*very softly at the window*]:
I wonder what's become of Sally, that old gal of mine?

[*He lowers the blind.*]

KILROY:
Well, anyhow . . .

THE BARON:
Well, anyhow?

KILROY:
How about the hot-spots in this town?

THE BARON:
Oh, the hot spots, ho ho! There's the Pink Flamingo, the Yellow Pelican, the Blue Heron, and the Prothonotary Warbler! They call it the Bird Circuit. But I don't care for such places. They stand three-deep at the bar and look at themselves in the mirror and what they see is depressing. One sailor comes in—they faint! My own choice of resorts is the

39

Bucket of Blood downstairs from the "Ritz Men Only."—
How about a match?

KILROY:

Where's your cigarette?

THE BARON [*gently and sweetly*]:

Oh, I don't smoke. I just wanted to see your eyes more
clearly . . .

KILROY:

Why?

THE BARON:

The eyes are the windows of the soul, and yours are too gentle
for someone who has as much as I have to atone for.

[*He starts off.*]
Au revoir . . .

KILROY:

—A very unusual type character . . .

[*Casanova is on the steps leading to the arch, looking out
at the desert beyond. Now he turns and descends a few
steps, laughing with a note of tired incredulity. Kilroy
crosses to him.*]

Gee, it's wonderful to see you, a normal American in a—

[*There is a strangulated outcry from the arch under which
the Baron has disappeared.*]

Excuse me a minute!

[*He rushes toward the source of the outcry. Jacques crosses
to the bench before the fountain. Rhubarb is heard through
the arch. Jacques shrugs wearily as if it were just a noisy*

radio. Kilroy comes plummeting out backward, all the way to Jacques.]

I tried to interfere, but what's th' use?!

JACQUES:
No use at all!

[*The Streetcleaners come through the arch with the Baron doubled up in their barrel. They pause and exchange sibilant whispers, pointing and snickering at Kilroy.*]

KILROY:
Who are they pointing at? At me, Kilroy?

[*The Bum laughs from the window. A. Ratt laughs from his shadowy doorway. The Loan Shark laughs from his.*]

Kilroy is here and he's not about to be there!—If he can help it . . .

[*He snatches up a rock and throws it at the Streetcleaners. Everybody laughs louder and the laughter seems to reverberate from the mountains. The light changes, dims a little in the plaza.*]

Sons a whatever you're sons of! Don't look at me, I'm not about to take no ride in the barrel!

[*The Baron, his elegant white shoes protruding from the barrel, is wheeled up the Alleyway Out. Figures in the square resume their dazed attitudes and one or two Guests return to the terrace of the Siete Mares as—*]

GUTMAN:
Block Five on the Camino Real!

[*He strolls off.*]

KILROY [*to Jacques*]:
Gee, the blocks go fast on this street!

JACQUES:
Yes. The blocks go fast.

KILROY:
My name's Kilroy. I'm here.

JACQUES:
Mine is Casanova. I'm here, too.

KILROY:
But you been here longer than me and maybe could brief me on it. For instance, what do they do with a stiff picked up in this town?

[*The Guard stares at them suspiciously from the terrace.*

[*Jacques whistles "La Golondrina" and crosses downstage. Kilroy follows.*]

Did I say something untactful?

JACQUES [*smiling into a sunset glow*]:
The exchange of serious questions and ideas, especially between persons from opposite sides of the plaza, is regarded unfavorably here. You'll notice I'm talking as if I had acute laryngitis. I'm gazing into the sunset. If I should start to whistle "La Golondrina" it means we're being overheard by the Guards on the terrace. Now you want to know what is done to a body from which the soul has departed on the Camino Real!—Its disposition depends on what the Street-cleaners happen to find in its pockets. If its pockets are empty as the unfortunate Baron's turned out to be, and as mine are at this moment—the "stiff" is wheeled straight off to the

Laboratory. And there the individual becomes an undistin-
guished member of a collectivist state. His chemical com-
ponents are separated and poured into vats containing the
corresponding elements of countless others. If any of his vital
organs or parts are at all unique in size or structure, they're
placed on exhibition in bottles containing a very foul-smelling
solution called formaldehyde. There is a charge of admission
to this museum. The proceeds go to the maintenance of the
military police.

[*He whistles "La Golondrina" till the Guard turns his back
again. He moves toward the front of the stage.*]

KILROY [*following*]:
—I guess that's—sensible . . .

JACQUES:
Yes, but not romantic. And romance is important. Don't you
think?

KILROY:
Nobody thinks romance is more important than me!

JACQUES:
Except possibly me!

KILROY:
Maybe that's why fate has brung us together! We're buddies
under the skin!

JACQUES:
Travelers born?

KILROY:
Always looking for something!

JACQUES:
Satisfied by nothing!

KILROY:

Hopeful?

JACQUES:

Always!

OFFICER:

Keep moving!

[*They move apart till the Officer exits.*]

KILROY:

And when a joker on the Camino gets fed up with one continual hassle—how does he get *off* it?

JACQUES:

You see the narrow and very steep stairway that passes under what is described in the travel brochures as a "Magnificent Arch of Triumph"?—Well, that's the Way Out!

KILROY:

That's the way out?

[*Kilroy without hesitation plunges right up to almost the top step; then pauses with a sound of squealing brakes. There is a sudden loud wind.*]

JACQUES [*shouting with hand cupped to mouth*]:

Well, how does the prospect please you, Traveler born?

KILROY [*shouting back in a tone of awe*]:

It's too unknown for my blood. Man, I seen nothing like it except through a telescope once on the pier on Coney Island. "Ten cents to see the craters and plains of the moon!"—And here's the same view in three dimensions for nothing!

[*The desert wind sings loudly: Kilroy mocks it.*]

44

JACQUES:

Are you—ready to cross it?

KILROY:

Maybe sometime with someone but not right now and alone!
How about you?

JACQUES:

I'm not alone.

KILROY:

You're with a party?

JACQUES:

No, but I'm sweetly encumbered with a—lady . . .

KILROY:

It wouldn't do with a lady. I don't see nothing but nothing—
and then more nothing. And then I see some mountains. But
the mountains are covered with snow.

JACQUES:

Snowshoes would be useful!

[*He observes Gutman approaching through the passage at
upper left. He whistles "La Golondrina" for Kilroy's attention and points with his cane as he exits.*]

KILROY [*descending steps disconsolately*]:
Mush, mush.

[*The Bum comes to his window. A. Ratt enters his doorway. Gutman enters below Kilroy.*]

BUM:

It's sleepy time down South!

GUTMAN [*warningly as Kilroy passes him*]:
Block Six in a progress of sixteen blocks on the Camino Real.

KILROY [*from the stairs*]:

Man, I could use a bed now.—I'd like to make me a cool pad on this camino now and lie down and sleep and dream of being with someone—friendly . . .

[*He crosses to the "Ritz Men Only."*]

A. RATT [*softly and sleepily*]:

Vacancy here! I got a single bed at the "Ritz Men Only," a little white ship to sail the dangerous night in.

[*Kilroy crosses down to his doorway.*]

KILROY:

—You got a vacancy here?

A. RATT:

I got a vacancy here if you got the one-fifty there.

KILROY:

Ha ha! I been in countries where money was not legal tender. I mean it was legal but it wasn't tender.

[*There is a loud groan from offstage above.*]

—Somebody dying on you or just drunk?

A. RATT:

Who knows or cares in this pad, Dad?

KILROY:

I heard once that a man can't die while he's drunk. Is that a fact or a fiction?

A. RATT:

Strictly a fiction.

VOICE ABOVE:

Stiff in number seven! Call the Streetcleaners!

A. RATT [*with absolutely no change in face or voice*]:
Number seven is vacant.

[*Streetcleaners' piping is heard.*

[*The Bum leaves the window.*]

KILROY:
Thanks, but tonight I'm going to sleep under the stars.

[*A. Ratt gestures "Have it your way" and exits.*

[*Kilroy, left alone, starts downstage. He notices that La Madrecita is crouched near the fountain, holding something up, inconspicuously, in her hand. Coming to her he sees that it's a piece of food. He takes it, puts it in his mouth, tries to thank her but her head is down, muffled in her rebozo and there is no way for him to acknowledge the gift. He starts to cross. Street People raise up their heads in their Pit and motion him invitingly to come in with them. They call softly, "Sleep, sleep . . ."*]

GUTMAN [*from his chair on the terrace*]:
Hey, Joe.

[*The Street People duck immediately.*]

KILROY:
Who? Me?

GUTMAN:
Yes, you, Candy Man. Are you disocupado?

KILROY:
—That means—unemployed, don't it?

[*He sees Officers converging from right.*]

GUTMAN:

Jobless. On the bum. Carrying the banner!

KILROY:

—Aw, no, aw, no, don't try to hang no vagrancy rap on me! I was robbed on this square and I got plenty of witnesses to prove it.

GUTMAN [*with ironic courtesy*]:

Oh?

[*He makes a gesture asking "Where?"*]

KILROY [*coming down to apron left and crossing to the right*]:

Witnesses! Witness! Witnesses!

[*He comes to La Madrecita.*]

You were a witness!

[*A gesture indicates that he realizes her blindness. Opposite the Gypsy's balcony he pauses for a second.*]

Hey, Gypsy's daughter!

[*The balcony is dark. He continues up to the Pit. The Street People duck as he calls down:*]

You were witnesses!

[*An Officer enters with a Patsy outfit. He hands it to Gutman.*]

GUTMAN:

Here, Boy! Take these.

[*Gutman displays and then tosses on the ground at Kilroy's feet the Patsy outfit—the red fright wig, the big crimson* nose that lights up and has horn-rimmed glasses attached, a pair of clown pants that have a huge footprint on the seat.]

KILROY:
What is this outfit?

GUTMAN:
The uniform of a Patsy.

KILROY:
I know what a Patsy is—he's a clown in the circus who takes pratfalls *but I'm no Patsy!*

GUTMAN:
Pick it up.

KILROY:
Don't give me orders. Kilroy is a free agent—

GUTMAN [*smoothly*]:
But a Patsy isn't. Pick it up and put it on, Candy Man. You are now the Patsy.

KILROY:
So you say but you are completely mistaken.

[*Four Officers press in on him.*]

And don't crowd me with your torpedoes! I'm a stranger here but I got a clean record in all the places I been, I'm not in the books for nothin' but vagrancy and once when I was hungry I walked by a truck-load of pineapples without picking one, because I was brought up good—

[*Then, with a pathetic attempt at making friends with the Officer to his right.*]

and there was a cop on the corner!

OFFICER:

Ponga selo!

KILROY:

What'd you say? [*Desperately to audience he asks:*] What did he say?

OFFICER:

Ponga selo!

KILROY:

What'd you say?

[*The Officer shoves him down roughly to the Patsy outfit. Kilroy picks up the pants, shakes them out carefully as if about to step into them and says very politely:*]

Why, surely. I'd be delighted. My fondest dreams have come true.

[*Suddenly he tosses the Patsy dress into Gutman's face and leaps into the aisle of the theatre.*]

GUTMAN:

Stop him! Arrest that vagrant! Don't let him get away!

LOUDSPEAKER:

Be on the lookout for a fugitive Patsy. The Patsy has escaped. Stop him, stop that Patsy!

[*A wild chase commences. The two Guards rush madly down either side to intercept him at the back of the house. Kilroy wheels about at the top of the center aisle, and runs back down it, panting, gasping out questions and entreaties to various persons occupying aisle seats, such as:*]

KILROY:

How do I git out? Which way do I go, which way do I get out? Where's the Greyhound depot? Hey, do you know

where the Greyhound bus depot is? What's the best way out,
if there is any way out? I got to find one. I had enough of
this place. I had too much of this place. I'm free. I'm a free
man with equal rights in this world! You better believe it
because that's news for you and you had better believe it!
Kilroy's a free man with equal rights in this world! All right,
now, help me, somebody, help me find a way out, I got to
find one, I don't like this place! It's not for me and I am not
buying any! Oh! Over there! I see a sign that says EXIT.
That's a sweet word to me, man, that's a lovely word, EXIT!
That's the entrance to paradise for Kilroy! Exit, I'm coming,
Exit, I'm coming!

[*The Street People have gathered along the forestage to
watch the chase. Esmeralda, barefooted, wearing only a slip,
bursts out of the Gypsy's establishment like an animal
broken out of a cage, darts among the Street People to the
front of the crowd which is shouting like the spectators at
the climax of a corrida. Behind her, Nursie appears, a male
actor, wigged and dressed austerely as a duenna, crying out
in both languages.*]

NURSIE:
Esmeralda! Esmeralda!

GYPSY:
Police!

NURSIE:
Come back here, Esmeralda!

GYPSY:
Catch her, idiot!

NURSIE:
Where is my lady bird, where is my precious treasure?

GYPSY:

Idiot! I told you to keep her door locked!

NURSIE:

She jimmied the lock, Esmeralda!

[*These shouts are mostly lost in the general rhubarb of the chase and the shouting Street People. Esmeralda crouches on the forestage, screaming encouragement in Spanish to the fugitive. Abdullah catches sight of her, seizes her wrist, shouting:*]

ABDULLAH:

Here she is! I got her!

[*Esmeralda fights savagely. She nearly breaks loose, but Nursie and the Gypsy close upon her, too, and she is overwhelmed and dragged back, fighting all the way, toward the door from which she escaped.*

[*Meanwhile—timed with the above action—shots are fired in the air by Kilroy's pursuers. He dashes, panting, into the boxes of the theatre, darting from one box to another, shouting incoherently, now, sobbing for breath, crying out:*]

KILROY:

Mary, help a Christian! Help a Christian, Mary!

ESMERALDA:

Yankee! Yankee, jump!

[*The Officers close upon him in the box nearest the stage. A dazzling spot of light is thrown on him. He lifts a little gilded chair to defend himself. The chair is torn from his grasp. He leaps upon the ledge of the box.*]

Jump! Jump, Yankee!

[*The Gypsy is dragging the girl back by her hair.*]

KILROY:

Watch out down there! Geronimo!

[*He leaps onto the stage and crumples up with a twisted ankle. Esmeralda screams demoniacally, breaks from her mother's grasp and rushes to him, fighting off his pursuers who have leapt after him from the box. Abdullah, Nursie and the Gypsy seize her again, just as Kilroy is seized by his pursuers. The Officers beat him to his knees. Each time he is struck, Esmeralda screams as if she received the blow herself. As his cries subside into sobbing, so do hers, and at the end, when he is quite helpless, she is also overcome by her captors and as they drag her back to the Gypsy's she cries to him:*]

ESMERALDA:

They've got you! They've got me!

[*Her mother slaps her fiercely.*]

Caught! Caught! We're caught!

[*She is dragged inside. The door is slammed shut on her continuing outcries. For a moment nothing is heard but Kilroy's hoarse panting and sobbing. Gutman takes command of the situation, thrusting his way through the crowd to face Kilroy who is pinioned by two Guards.*]

GUTMAN [*smiling serenely*]:

Well, well, how do you do! I understand that you're seeking employment here. We need a Patsy and the job is yours for the asking!

KILROY:

I don't. Accept. This job. I been. Shanghied!

[*Kilroy dons Patsy outfit.*]

GUTMAN:

Hush! The Patsy doesn't talk. He lights his nose, that's all!

GUARD:

Press the little button at the end of the cord.

GUTMAN:

That's right. Just press the little button at the end of the cord!

[*Kilroy lights his nose. Everybody laughs.*]

GUTMAN:

Again, ha ha! Again, ha ha! Again!

[*The nose goes off and on like a firefly as the stage dims out.*

[*The curtain falls. There is a short intermission.*]

BLOCK SEVEN

*The Dreamer is singing with mandolin, "Noche de Ronde."
The Guests murmur, "cool—cool . . ." Gutman stands on the
podiumlike elevation downstage right, smoking a long thin
cigar, signing an occasional tab from the bar or café. He is
standing in an amber spot. The rest of the stage is filled with
blue dusk. At the signal the song fades to a whisper and
Gutman speaks.*

GUTMAN:
Block Seven on the Camino Real—
I like this hour.

[*He gives the audience a tender gold-toothed smile.*]

The fire's gone out of the day but the light of it lingers . . .
In Rome the continual fountains are bathing stone heroes with
silver, in Copenhagen the Tivoli Gardens are lighted, they're
selling the lottery on San Juan de Latrene . . .

[*The Dreamer advances a little, playing the mandolin
softly.*]

LA MADRECITA [*holding up glass beads and shell necklaces*]:
Recuerdos, recuerdos?

GUTMAN:
And these are the moments when we look into ourselves and
ask with a wonder which never is lost altogether: "Can this
be all? Is there nothing more? Is this what the glittering
wheels of the heavens turn for?"

[*He leans forward as if conveying a secret.*]

—Ask the Gypsy! Un poco dinero will tickle the Gypsy's palm
and give her visions!

[*Abdullah emerges with a silver tray, calling:*]

ABDULLAH:
Letter for Signor Casanova, letter for Signor Casanova!

[*Jacques springs up but stands rigid.*]

GUTMAN:
Casanova, you have received a letter. Perhaps it's the letter with the remittance check in it!

JACQUES [*in a hoarse, exalted voice*]:
Yes! It is! The letter! With the remittance check in it!

GUTMAN:
Then why don't you take it so you can maintain your residence at the Siete Mares and so avoid the more somber attractions of the "Ritz Men Only"?

JACQUES:
My hand is—

GUTMAN:
Your hand is paralyzed? . . . By what? *Anxiety? Apprehension?* . . . Put the letter in Signor Casanova's pocket so he can open it when he recovers the use of his digital extremities. Then give him a shot of brandy on the house before he falls on his face!

[*Jacques has stepped down into the plaza. He looks down at Kilroy crouched to the right of him and wildly blinking his nose.*]

JACQUES:
Yes. I know the Morse code.

[*Kilroy's nose again blinks on and off.*]

Thank you, brother.

[*This is said as if acknowledging a message.*]

I knew without asking the Gypsy that something of this sort would happen to you. You have a spark of anarchy in your spirit and that's not to be tolerated. Nothing wild or honest is tolerated here! It has to be extinguished or used only to light up your nose for Mr. Gutman's amusement . . .

[Jacques saunters around Kilroy whistling "La Golondrina." Then satisfied that no one is suspicious of this encounter . . .]

Before the final block we'll find some way out of here! Meanwhile, patience and courage, little brother!

[Jacques feeling he's been there too long starts away giving Kilroy a reassuring pat on the shoulder and saying:]

Patience! . . . Courage!

LADY MULLIGAN *[from the Mulligans' table]*:
Mr. Gutman!

GUTMAN:
Lady Mulligan! And how are you this evening, Lord Mulligan?

LADY MULLIGAN *[interrupting Lord Mulligan's rumblings]*:
He's not at all well. This . . . climate is so enervating!

LORD MULLIGAN:
I was so weak this morning . . . I couldn't screw the lid on my tooth paste!

LADY MULLIGAN:
Raymond, tell Mr. Gutman about those two impertinent workmen in the square! . . . These two idiots pushing a white barrel! Pop up every time we step outside the hotel!

LORD MULLIGAN:
—point and giggle at me!

57

LADY MULLIGAN:

Can't they be discharged?

GUTMAN:

They can't be discharged, disciplined nor bribed! All you can
do is pretend to ignore them.

LADY MULLIGAN:

I can't eat! . . . Raymond, stop stuffing!

LORD MULLIGAN:

Shut up!

GUTMAN [*to the audience*]:

When the big wheels crack on this street it's like the fall of
a capital city, the destruction of Carthage, the sack of Rome
by the white-eyed giants from the North! I've seen them fall!
I've seen the destruction of them! Adventurers suddenly
frightened of a dark room! Gamblers unable to choose between odd and even! Con men and pitchmen and plume-
hatted cavaliers turned baby-soft at one note of the Streetcleaners' pipes! When I observe this change, I say to myself:
"Could it happen to ME?"—The answer is "YES!" And
that's what curdles my blood like milk on the doorstep of
someone gone for the summer!

[*A Hunchback Mummer somersaults through his hoop of
silver bells, springs up and shakes it excitedly toward a
downstage arch which begins to flicker with a diamond-
blue radiance; this marks the advent of each legendary
character in the play. The music follows: a waltz from the
time of Camille in Paris.*]

GUTMAN [*downstage to the audience*]:

Ah, there's the music of another legend, one that everyone
knows, the legend of the sentimental whore, the courtesan

who made the mistake of love. But now you see her coming into this plaza not as she was when she burned with a fever that cast a thin light over Paris, but changed, yes, faded as lanterns and legends fade when they burn into day!

[*He turns and shouts:*]

Rosita, sell her a flower!

[*Marguerite has entered the plaza. A beautiful woman of indefinite age. The Street People cluster about her with wheedling cries, holding up glass beads, shell necklaces and so forth. She seems confused, lost, half-awake. Jacques has sprung up at her entrance but has difficulty making his way through the cluster of vendors. Rosita has snatched up a tray of flowers and cries out:*]

ROSITA:
Camellias, camellias! Pink or white, whichever a lady finds suitable to the moon!

GUTMAN:
That's the ticket!

MARGUERITE:
Yes, I would like a camellia.

ROSITA [*in a bad French accent*]:
Rouge ou blanc ce soir?

MARGUERITE:
It's always a white one, now . . . but there used to be five evenings out of the month when a pink camellia, instead of the usual white one, let my admirers know that the moon those nights was unfavorable to pleasure, and so they called me—Camille . . .

59

JACQUES:
Mia cara!

[*Imperiously, very proud to be with her, he pushes the Street People aside with his cane.*]

Out of the way, make way, let us through, please!

MARGUERITE:
Don't push them with your cane.

JACQUES:
If they get close enough they'll snatch your purse.

[*Marguerite utters a low, shocked cry.*]

What is it?

MARGUERITE:
My purse is gone! It's lost! My papers were in it!

JACQUES:
Your passport was in it?

MARGUERITE:
My passport and my permiso de residencia!

[*She leans faint against the arch during the following scene.*

[*Abdullah turns to run. Jacques catches him.*]

JACQUES [*seizing Abdullah's wrist*]:
Where did you take her?

ABDULLAH:
Oww!—P'tit Zoco.

JACQUES:
The Souks?

ABDULLAH:
The Souks!

JACQUES:
Which cafés did she go to?

ABDULLAH:
Ahmed's, she went to—

JACQUES:
Did she smoke at Ahmed's?

ABDULLAH:
Two kif pipes!

JACQUES:
Who was it took her purse? Was it *you*? We'll see!

[*He strips off the boy's burnoose. He crouches whimpering, shivering in a ragged slip.*]

MARGUERITE:
Jacques, let the boy go, he didn't take it!

JACQUES:
He doesn't have it on him but knows who does!

ABDULLAH:
No, no, I don't know!

JACQUES:
You little son of a Gypsy! Senta! . . . You know who I am? I am Jacques Casanova! I belong to the Secret Order of the Rose-colored Cross! . . . Run back to Ahmed's. Contact the spiv that took the lady's purse. Tell him to keep it but give her back her papers! There'll be a large reward.

[*He thumps his cane on the ground to release Abdullah*

*from the spell. The boy dashes off. Jacques laughs and turns
triumphantly to Marguerite.*]

LADY MULLIGAN:
Waiter! That adventurer and his mistress must not be seated
next to Lord Mulligan's table!

JACQUES [*loudly enough for Lady Mulligan to hear*]:
This hotel has become a mecca for black marketeers and their
expensively kept women!

LADY MULLIGAN:
Mr. Gutman!

MARGUERITE:
Let's have dinner upstairs!

WAITER [*directing them to terrace table*]:
This way, M'sieur.

JACQUES:
We'll take our usual table.

[*He indicates one.*]

MARGUERITE:
Please!

WAITER [*overlapping Marguerite's "Please!"*]:
This table is reserved for Lord Byron!

JACQUES [*masterfully*]:
This table is always our table.

MARGUERITE:
I'm not hungry.

JACQUES:
Hold out the lady's chair, cretino!

62

GUTMAN [*darting over to Marguerite's chair*]:
Permit me!

[*Jacques bows with mock gallantry to Lady Mulligan as he turns to his chair during seating of Marguerite.*]

LADY MULLIGAN:
We'll move to *that* table!

JACQUES:
—You must learn how to carry the banner of Bohemia into the enemy camp.

[*A screen is put up around them.*]

MARGUERITE:
Bohemia has no banner. It survives by discretion.

JACQUES:
I'm glad that you value discretion. *Wine list!* Was it discretion that led you through the bazaars this afternoon wearing your cabochon sapphire and diamond eardrops? You were fortunate that you lost only your purse and papers!

MARGUERITE:
Take the wine list.

JACQUES:
Still or sparkling?

MARGUERITE:
Sparkling.

GUTMAN:
May I make a suggestion, Signor Casanova?

JACQUES:
Please do.

GUTMAN:

It's a very cold and dry wine from only ten metres below the snowline in the mountains. The name of the wine is Quando! —meaning when! Such as "When are remittances going to be received?" "When are accounts to be settled?" Ha ha ha! Bring Signor Casanova a bottle of Quando with the compliments of the house!

JACQUES:

I'm sorry this had to happen in—your presence . . .

MARGUERITE:

That doesn't matter, my dear. But why don't you *tell* me when you are short of money?

JACQUES:

I thought the fact was apparent. It is to everyone else.

MARGUERITE:

The letter you were expecting, it still hasn't come?

JACQUES [*removing it from his pocket*]:
It came this afternoon—Here it is!

MARGUERITE:

You haven't opened the letter!

JACQUES:

I haven't had the nerve to! I've had so many unpleasant surprises that I've lost faith in my luck.

MARGUERITE:

Give the letter to me. Let me open it for you.

JACQUES:

Later, a little bit later, after the—wine . . . ·

64

MARGUERITE:
Old hawk, anxious old hawk!

[*She clasps his hand on the table; he leans toward her; she kisses her fingertips and places them on his lips.*]

JACQUES:
Do you call that a kiss?

MARGUERITE:
I call it the ghost of a kiss. It will have to do for now.

[*She leans back, her blue-tinted eyelids closed.*]

JACQUES:
Are you tired? Are you tired, Marguerite? You know you should have rested this afternoon.

MARGUERITE:
I looked at silver and rested.

JACQUES:
You looked at silver at Ahmed's?

MARGUERITE:
No, I rested at Ahmed's, and had mint tea.

[*The Dreamer accompanies their speech with his guitar. The duologue should have the style of an antiphonal poem, the cues picked up so that there is scarcely a separation between the speeches, and the tempo quick and the voices edged.*]

JACQUES:
You had mint tea downstairs?

MARGUERITE:
No, upstairs.

JACQUES:

Upstairs where they burn the poppy?

MARGUERITE:

Upstairs where it's cool and there's music and the haggling of the bazaar is soft as the murmur of pigeons.

JACQUES:

That sounds restful. Reclining among silk pillows on a divan, in a curtained and perfumed alcove above the bazaar?

MARGUERITE:

Forgetting for a while where I am, or that I don't know where I am . . .

JACQUES:

Forgetting alone or forgetting with some young companion who plays the lute or the flute or who had silver to show you? Yes. That sounds very restful. And yet you do seem tired.

MARGUERITE:

If I seem tired, it's your insulting solicitude that I'm tired of!

JACQUES:

Is it insulting to feel concern for your safety in this place?

MARGUERITE:

Yes, it is. The implication is.

JACQUES:

What is the implication?

MARGUERITE:

You know what it is: that I am one of those *aging—voluptuaries*—who used to be paid for pleasure but now have to pay!—Jacques, I won't be followed, I've gone too far to be followed!—*What is it?*

[*The Waiter has presented an envelope on a salver.*]

WAITER:

A letter for the lady.

MARGUERITE:

How strange to receive a letter in a place where nobody knows I'm staying! Will you open it for me?

[*The Waiter withdraws. Jacques takes the letter and opens it.*]

Well! What is it?

JACQUES:

Nothing important. An illustrated brochure from some resort in the mountains.

MARGUERITE:

What is it called?

JACQUES:

Bide-a-While.

[*A chafing dish bursts into startling blue flame at the Mulligans' table. Lady Mulligan clasps her hands and exclaims with affected delight, the Waiter and Mr. Gutman laugh agreeably. Marguerite springs up and moves out upon the forestage. Jacques goes to her.*]

Do you know this resort in the mountains?

MARGUERITE:

Yes. I stayed there once. It's one of those places with open sleeping verandahs, surrounded by snowy pine woods. It has rows and rows of narrow white iron beds as regular as tombstones. The invalids smile at each other when axes flash across valleys, ring, flash, ring again! Young voices shout across

67

valleys Hola! And mail is delivered. The friend that used to write you ten-page letters contents himself now with a post card bluebird that tells you to "Get well quick!"

[*Jacques throws the brochure away.*]

—And when the last bleeding comes, not much later nor earlier than expected, you're wheeled discreetly into a little tent of white gauze, and the last thing you know of this world, of which you've known so little and yet so much, is the smell of an empty icebox.

[*The blue flame expires in the chafing dish. Gutman picks up the brochure and hands it to the Waiter, whispering something.*]

JACQUES:
You won't go back to that place.

[*The Waiter places the brochure on the salver again and approaches behind them.*]

MARGUERITE:
I wasn't released. I left without permission. They sent me this to remind me.

WAITER [*presenting the salver*]:
You dropped this.

JACQUES:
We threw it away!

WAITER:
Excuse me.

JACQUES:
Now, from now on, Marguerite, you must take better care of yourself. Do you hear me?

68

MARGUERITE:

I hear you. No more distractions for me? No more entertainers in curtained and perfumed alcoves above the bazaar, no more young men that a pinch of white powder or a puff of gray smoke can almost turn to someone devoutly remembered?

JACQUES:

No, from now on—

MARGUERITE:

What "from now on," old hawk?

JACQUES:

Rest. Peace.

MARGUERITE:

Rest in peace is that final bit of advice they carve on gravestones, and I'm not ready for it! Are you? Are *you* ready for it?

[*She returns to the table. He follows her.*]

Oh, Jacques, when are we going to leave here, how are we going to leave here, you've got to tell me!

JACQUES:

I've told you all I know.

MARGUERITE:

Nothing, you've given up hope!

JACQUES:

I haven't, that's not true.

[*Gutman has brought out the white cockatoo which he shows to Lady Mulligan at her table.*]

GUTMAN [*his voice rising above the murmurs*]:
Her name is Aurora.

69

LADY MULLIGAN:
Why do you call her Aurora?

GUTMAN:
She cries at daybreak.

LADY MULLIGAN:
Only at daybreak?

GUTMAN:
Yes, at daybreak only.

[*Their voices and laughter fade under.*]

MARGUERITE:
How long is it since you've been to the travel agencies?

JACQUES:
This morning I made the usual round of Cook's, American Express, Wagon-lits Universal, and it was the same story. There are no flights out of here till further orders from someone higher up.

MARGUERITE:
Nothing, nothing at all?

JACQUES:
Oh, there's a rumor of something called the Fugitivo, but—

MARGUERITE:
The What!!! ?

JACQUES:
The Fugitivo. It's one of those nonscheduled things that—

MARGUERITE:
When, when, when?

JACQUES:

I told you it was nonscheduled. Nonscheduled means it comes and goes at no predictable—

MARGUERITE:

Don't give me the dictionary! I want to know how does one get on it? Did you bribe them? Did you offer them money? No. Of course you didn't! And I know why! You really don't want to leave here. You *think* you don't want to go because you're brave as an old hawk. But the truth of the matter—the real not the royal truth—is that you're terrified of the Terra Incognita outside that wall.

JACQUES:

You've hit upon the truth. I'm terrified of the unknown country inside or outside this wall or any place on earth without you with me! The only country, known or unknown that I can breathe in, or care to, is the country in which we breathe together, as we are now at this table. And later, a little while later, even closer than this, the sole inhabitants of a tiny world whose limits are those of the light from a rose-colored lamp— beside the sweetly, completely known country of your cool bed!

MARGUERITE:

The little comfort of love?

JACQUES:

Is that comfort so little?

MARGUERITE:

Caged birds accept each other but flight is what they long for.

JACQUES:

I want to stay here with you and love you and guard you

until the time or way comes that we both can leave with honor.

MARGUERITE:

"Leave with honor"? Your vocabulary is almost as out-of-date as your cape and your cane. How could anyone quit this field with honor, this place where there's nothing but the gradual wasting away of everything decent in us . . . the sort of desperation that comes after even desperation has been worn out through long wear! . . . Why have they put these screens around the table?

[*She springs up and knocks one of them over.*]

LADY MULLIGAN:

There! You see? I don't understand why you let such people stay here.

GUTMAN:

They pay the price of admission the same as you.

LADY MULLIGAN:

What price is that?

GUTMAN:

Desperation!—With cash here!

[*He indicates the Siete Mares.*]

Without cash there!

[*He indicates Skid Row.*]

Block Eight on the Camino Real!

BLOCK EIGHT

*There is the sound of loud desert wind and a flamenco cry
followed by a dramatic phrase of music.*

*A flickering diamond-blue radiance floods the hotel entrance.
The crouching, grimacing Hunchback shakes his hoop of
bells which is the convention for the appearance of each
legendary figure.*

*Lord Byron appears in the doorway readied for departure.
Gutman raises his hand for silence.*

GUTMAN:
You're leaving us, Lord Byron?

BYRON:
Yes, I'm leaving you, Mr. Gutman.

GUTMAN:
What a pity! But this is a port of entry and departure. There
are no permanent guests. Possibly you are getting a little
restless?

BYRON:
The luxuries of this place have made me soft. The metal
point's gone from my pen, there's nothing left but the feather.

GUTMAN:
That may be true. But what can you do about it?

BYRON:
Make a departure!

GUTMAN:
From yourself?

BYRON:
From my present self to myself as I used to be!

GUTMAN:

That's the *furthest* departure a man could make! I guess you're sailing to Athens? There's another war there and like all wars since the beginning of time it can be interpreted as a —struggle for *what?*

BYRON:

—For *freedom!* You may laugh at it, but it still means something to *me!*

GUTMAN:

Of course it does! I'm not laughing a bit, I'm beaming with admiration.

BYRON:

I've allowed myself many distractions.

GUTMAN:

Yes, indeed!

BYRON:

But I've never altogether forgotten my old devotion to the—

GUTMAN:

—To the *what,* Lord Byron?

[*Byron passes nervous fingers through his hair.*]

You can't remember the object of your one-time devotion?

[*There is a pause. Byron limps away from the terrace and goes toward the fountain.*]

BYRON:

When Shelley's corpse was recovered from the sea . . .

[*Gutman beckons the Dreamer who approaches and accompanies Byron's speech.*]

—It was burned on the beach at Viareggio.—I watched the spectacle from my carriage because the stench was revolting . . . Then it—fascinated me! I got out of my carriage. Went nearer, holding a handkerchief to my nostrils!—I saw that the front of the skull had broken away in the flames, and there—

[*He advances out upon the stage apron, followed by Abdullah with the pine torch or lantern.*]

And there was the brain of Shelley, indistinguishable from a cooking stew!—*boiling, bubbling, hissing!*—in the *blackening —cracked—pot—*of his skull!

[*Marguerite rises abruptly. Jacques supports her.*]

—Trelawney, his friend, Trelawney, threw salt and oil and frankincense in the flames and finally the almost intolerable stench—

[*Abdullah giggles. Gutman slaps him.*]

—was *gone* and the burning was *pure!*—as a man's burning should be . . .

A man's burning *ought* to be pure!—*not* like mine—(a crepe suzette—burned in brandy . . .)

Shelley's burning was finally very *pure!*

But the body, the corpse, split open like a grilled pig!

[*Abdullah giggles irrepressibly again. Gutman grips the back of his neck and he stands up stiff and assumes an expression of exaggerated solemnity.*]

—And then Trelawney—as the ribs of the corpse unlocked— reached into them as a baker reaches quickly into an oven!

[Abdullah almost goes into another convulsion.]

—And snatched out—as a baker would a biscuit!—the *heart* of Shelley! Snatched the heart of Shelley out of the blistering corpse!—Out of the purifying—blue flame . . .

[Marguerite resumes her seat; Jacques his.]

—And it was *over!*—I thought—

[He turns slightly from the audience and crosses upstage from the apron. He faces Jacques and Marguerite.]

—I thought it was a disgusting thing to do, to snatch a man's heart from his body! What can one man do with another man's heart?

[Jacques rises and strikes the stage with his cane.]

JACQUES *[passionately]*:
He can do this with it!

[He seizes a loaf of bread on his table, and descends from the terrace.]

He can twist it like this!

[He twists the loaf.]

He can tear it like this!

[He tears the loaf in two.]

He can crush it under his foot!

[He drops the bread and stamps on it.]

—And kick it away—like this!

[He kicks the bread off the terrace. Lord Byron turns away from him and limps again out upon the stage apron and speaks to the audience.]

BYRON:

That's very true, Señor. But a poet's vocation, which used to be my vocation, is to influence the heart in a gentler fashion than you have made your mark on that loaf of bread. He ought to purify it and lift it above its ordinary level. For what is the heart but a sort of—

[*He makes a high, groping gesture in the air.*]

—A sort of—*instrument!*—that translates *noise* into *music, chaos* into—*order* . . .

[*Abdullah ducks almost to the earth in an effort to stifle his mirth. Gutman coughs to cover his own amusement.*]

—a mysterious order!

[*He raises his voice till it fills the plaza.*]

—That was my vocation once upon a time, before it was obscured by vulgar plaudits!—Little by little it was lost among gondolas and palazzos!—masked balls, glittering salons, huge shadowy courts and torch-lit entrances!—Baroque façades, canopies and carpets, candelabra and gold plate among snowy damask, ladies with throats as slender as flower stems, bending and breathing toward me their fragrant breath—

—Exposing their breasts to me!

Whispering, half smiling!—And everywhere marble, the visible grandeur of marble, pink and gray marble, veined and tinted as flayed corrupting flesh,—all these provided agreeable distractions from the rather frightening solitude of a poet. Oh, I wrote many cantos in Venice and Constantinople and in Ravenna and Rome, on all of those Latin and Levantine excursions that my twisted foot led me into—but I wonder about them a little. They seem to improve as the wine in the bottle—dwindles . . . *There is a passion for declivity in this world!*

And lately I've found myself listening to hired musicians behind a row of artificial palm trees—instead of the single—pure-stringed instrument of my heart . . .

Well, then, it's time to leave here!

[*He turns back to the stage.*]

—There is a time for departure even when there's no certain place to go!

I'm going to look for one, now. I'm sailing to Athens. At least I can look up at the Acropolis, I can stand at the foot of it and look up at broken columns on the crest of a hill—if not purity, at least its recollection . . .

I can sit quietly looking for a long, long time in absolute silence, and possibly, yes, *still* possibly—

The old pure music will come to me again. Of course on the other hand I may hear only the little noise of insects in the grass . . .

But I am sailing to Athens! *Make voyages!—Attempt them!—* there's nothing else . . .

MARGUERITE [*excitedly*]:
Watch where he goes!

[*Lord Byron limps across the plaza with his head bowed, making slight, apologetic gestures to the wheedling Beggars who shuffle about him. There is music. He crosses toward the steep Alleyway Out. The following is played with a quiet intensity so it will be in a lower key than the later Fugitivo Scene.*]

Watch him, watch him, see which way he goes. Maybe he knows of a way that we haven't found out.

JACQUES:

Yes, I'm watching him, cara.

[*Lord and Lady Mulligan half rise, staring anxiously through monocle and lorgnon.*]

MARGUERITE:

Oh, my God, I believe he's going up that alley.

JACQUES:

Yes, he is. He has.

LORD and LADY MULLIGAN:

Oh, the fool, the idiot, he's going under the arch!

MARGUERITE:

Jacques, run after him, warn him, tell him about the desert he has to cross.

JACQUES:

I think he knows what he's doing.

MARGUERITE:

I can't look!

[*She turns to the audience, throwing back her head and closing her eyes. The desert wind sings loudly as Byron climbs to the top of the steps.*]

BYRON [*to several porters carrying luggage—which is mainly caged birds*]:

THIS WAY!

[*He exits.*

[*Kilroy starts to follow. He stops at the steps, cringing and*

79

looking at Gutman. Gutman motions him to go ahead. Kilroy rushes up the stairs. He looks out, loses his nerve and sits—blinking his nose. Gutman laughs as he announces—]

GUTMAN:
Block Nine on the Camino Real!

[*He goes into the hotel.*]

BLOCK NINE

Abdullah runs back to the hotel with the billowing flambeau.
A faint and faraway humming sound becomes audible . . .
Marguerite opens her eyes with a startled look. She searches
the sky for something. A very low percussion begins with the
humming sound, as if excited hearts are beating.

MARGUERITE:
Jacques! I hear something in the sky!

JACQUES:
I think what you hear is—

MARGUERITE [*with rising excitement*]:
—No, it's a plane, a great one, I see the lights of it, now!

JACQUES:
Some kind of fireworks, cara.

MARGUERITE:
Hush! LISTEN!

[*She blows out the candle to see better above it. She rises,*
peering into the sky.]

I see it! I see it! There! It's circling over us!

LADY MULLIGAN:
Raymond, Raymond, sit down, your face is flushed!

HOTEL GUESTS [*overlapping*]:
—What is it?
—The FUGITIVO!
—THE FUGITIVO! THE FUGITIVO!
—Quick, get my jewelry from the hotel safe!
—Cash a check!

—Throw some things in a bag! I'll wait here!
—Never mind luggage, we have our money and papers!
—Where is it now?
—There, there!
—It's turning to land!
—To go like this?
—Yes, go anyhow, just go anyhow, just go!
—Raymond! Please!
—Oh, it's rising again!
—Oh, it's—*SHH! MR. GUTMAN!*

[*Gutman appears in the doorway. He raises a hand in a commanding gesture.*]

GUTMAN:

Signs in the sky should not be mistaken for wonders!

[*The Voices modulate quickly.*]

Ladies, gentlemen, please resume your seats!

[*Places are resumed at tables, and silver is shakily lifted. Glasses are raised to lips, but the noise of concerted panting of excitement fills the stage and a low percussion echoes frantic heart beats.*

[*Gutman descends to the plaza, shouting furiously to the Officer.*]

Why wasn't I told the Fugitivo was coming?

[*Everyone, almost as a man, rushes into the hotel and reappears almost at once with hastily collected possessions. Marguerite rises but appears stunned.*

[*There is a great whistling and screeching sound as the aerial transport halts somewhere close by, accompanied by rainbow splashes of light and cries like children's on a*

82

*roller coaster. Some incoming Passengers approach the stage
down an aisle of the theatre, preceded by Redcaps with luggage.*]

PASSENGERS:
—What a heavenly trip!
—The scenery was thrilling!
—It's so quick!
—The only way to travel! Etc., etc.

[*A uniformed man, the Pilot, enters the plaza with a
megaphone.*]

PILOT [*through the megaphone*]:
Fugitivo now loading for departure! Fugitivo loading immediately for departure! Northwest corner of the plaza!

MARGUERITE:
Jacques, it's the Fugitivo, it's the nonscheduled thing you
heard of this afternoon!

PILOT:
All out-going passengers on the Fugitivo are requested to
present their tickets and papers immediately at this station.

MARGUERITE:
He said "outgoing passengers"!

PILOT:
Outgoing passengers on the Fugitivo report immediately at
this station for customs inspection.

MARGUERITE [*with a forced smile*]:
Why are you just standing there?

JACQUES [*with an Italian gesture*]:
Che cosa possa fare!

MARGUERITE:

Move, move, do something!

JACQUES:

What!

MARGUERITE:

Go to them, ask, find out!

JACQUES:

I have no idea what the damned thing is!

MARGUERITE:

I do, I'll tell you! It's a way to escape from this abominable place!

JACQUES:

Forse, forse, non so!

MARGUERITE:

It's a way *out* and *I'm* not going to miss it!

PILOT:

Ici la Douane! Customs inspection here!

MARGUERITE:

Customs. That means luggage. Run to my room! Here! Key! Throw a few things in a bag, my jewels, my furs, but hurry! Vite, vite, vite! I don't believe there's much time! No, everybody is—

[*Outgoing Passengers storm the desk and table.*]

—Clamoring for tickets! There must be limited space! Why don't you do what I tell you?

[*She rushes to a man with a rubber stamp and a roll of tickets.*]

Monsieur! Señor! Pardonnez-moi! I'm going, I'm going out!
I want my ticket!

PILOT [*coldly*]:
Name, please.

MARGUERITE:
Mademoiselle—Gautier—but I—

PILOT:
Gautier? Gautier? We have no Gautier listed.

MARGUERITE:
I'm—*not* listed! I mean I'm—traveling under another name.

TRAVEL AGENT:
What name are you traveling under?

[*Prudence and Olympe rush out of the hotel half dressed,
dragging their furs. Meanwhile Kilroy is trying to make a
fast buck or two as a Redcap. The scene gathers wild momentum, is punctuated by crashes of percussion. Grotesque
mummers act as demon custom inspectors and immigration
authorities, etc. Baggage is tossed about, ripped open, smug-
gled goods seized, arrests made, all amid the wildest im-
portunities, protests, threats, bribes, entreaties; it is a scene
for improvisation.*]

PRUDENCE:
Thank God I woke up!

OLYMPE:
Thank God I wasn't asleep!

PRUDENCE:
I knew it was nonscheduled but I *did* think they'd give you
time to get in your girdle.

OLYMPE:
Look who's trying to crash it! I know damned well *she* don't have a reservation!

PILOT [*to Marguerite*]:
What name did you say, Mademoiselle? Please! People are waiting, you're holding up the line!

MARGUERITE:
I'm so confused! Jacques! What name did you make my reservation under?

OLYMPE:
She has no reservation!

PRUDENCE:
I have, I got mine!

OLYMPE:
I got mine!

PRUDENCE:
I'm next!

OLYMPE:
Don't push *me*, you old bag!

MARGUERITE:
I was here first! I was here before anybody! Jacques, quick! Get my money from the hotel safe!

[*Jacques exits.*]

AGENT:
Stay in line!

[*There is a loud warning whistle.*]

PILOT:

Five minutes. The Fugitivo leaves in five minutes. Five, five minutes only!

[*At this announcement the scene becomes riotous.*]

TRAVEL AGENT:

Four minutes! The Fugitivo leaves in four minutes!

[*Prudence and Olympe are shrieking at him in French. The warning whistle blasts again.*]

Three minutes, the Fugitivo leaves in three minutes!

MARGUERITE [*topping the turmoil*]:

Monsieur! Please! I was here first, I was here before anybody! Look!

[*Jacques returns with her money.*]

I have thousands of francs! Take whatever you want! Take all of it, it's yours!

PILOT:

Payment is only accepted in pounds sterling or dollars. Next, please.

MARGUERITE:

You don't accept francs? They do at the hotel! They accept my francs at the Siete Mares!

PILOT:

Lady, don't argue with me, I don't make the rules!

MARGUERITE [*beating her forehead with her fist*]:

Oh, God, Jacques! Take these back to the cashier!

[*She thrusts the bills at him.*]

Get them changed to dollars or—*Hurry! Tout de suite!* I'm—going to faint ...

JACQUES:
But Marguerite—

MARGUERITE:
Go! Go! Please!

PILOT:
Closing, we're closing now! The Fugitivo leaves in two minutes!

[*Lord and Lady Mulligan rush forward.*]

LADY MULLIGAN:
Let Lord Mulligan through.

PILOT [*to Marguerite*]:
You're standing in the way.

[*Olympe screams as the Customs Inspector dumps her jewels on the ground. She and Prudence butt heads as they dive for the gems: the fight is renewed.*]

MARGUERITE [*detaining the Pilot*]:
Oh, look, Monsieur! Regardez ça! My diamond, a solitaire—two carats! Take that as security!

PILOT:
Let me go. The Loan Shark's across the plaza!

[*There is another warning blast. Prudence and Olympe seize hat boxes and rush toward the whistle.*]

MARGUERITE [*clinging desperately to the Pilot*]:
You don't understand! Señor Casanova has gone to change money! He'll be here in a second. And I'll pay five, ten, twenty

times the price of—*JACQUES! JACQUES! WHERE ARE YOU?*

VOICE [*back of auditorium*]:
We're closing the gate!

MARGUERITE:
You can't close the gate!

PILOT:
Move, Madame!

MARGUERITE:
I won't move!

LADY MULLIGAN:
I tell you, Lord Mulligan is the Iron & Steel man from Cobh!
Raymond! They're closing the gate!

LORD MULLIGAN:
I can't seem to get through!

GUTMAN:
Hold the gate for Lord Mulligan!

PILOT [*to Marguerite*]:
Madame, stand back or I will have to use force!

MARGUERITE:
Jacques! Jacques!

LADY MULLIGAN:
Let us through! We're clear!

PILOT:
Madame! Stand back and let these passengers through!

MARGUERITE:
No, No! I'm first! I'm next!

LORD MULLIGAN:
Get her out of our way! That woman's a whore!

LADY MULLIGAN:
How dare you stand in our way?

PILOT:
Officer, take this woman!

LADY MULLIGAN:
Come on, Raymond!

MARGUERITE [*as the Officer pulls her away*]:
Jacques! Jacques! Jacques!

[*Jacques returns with changed money.*]

Here! Here is the money!

PILOT:
All right, give me your papers.

MARGUERITE:
—My papers? Did you say my papers?

PILOT:
Hurry, hurry, your passport!

MARGUERITE:
—Jacques! He wants my papers! Give him my papers, Jacques!

JACQUES:
—The lady's papers are lost!

MARGUERITE [*wildly*]:
No, no, no, THAT IS NOT TRUE! HE WANTS TO KEEP ME HERE! HE'S LYING ABOUT IT!

90

JACQUES:
Have you forgotten that your papers were stolen?

MARGUERITE:
I gave you my papers, I gave you my papers to keep, you've got my papers.

[*Screaming, Lady Mulligan breaks past her and descends the stairs.*]

LADY MULLIGAN:
Raymond! Hurry!

LORD MULLIGAN [*staggering on the top step*]:
I'm sick! I'm sick!

[*The Streetcleaners disguised as expensive morticians in swallowtail coats come rapidly up the aisle of the theatre and wait at the foot of the stairway for the tottering tycoon.*]

LADY MULLIGAN:
You cannot be sick till we get on the Fugitivo!

LORD MULLIGAN:
Forward all cables to Guaranty Trust in Paris.

LADY MULLIGAN:
Place de la Concorde.

LORD MULLIGAN:
Thank you! All purchases C.O.D. to Mulligan Iron & Steel Works in Cobh—Thank you!

LADY MULLIGAN:
Raymond! Raymond! Who are these men?

LORD MULLIGAN:
I know these men! I recognize their faces!

LADY MULLIGAN:

Raymond! They're the Streetcleaners!

[*She screams and runs up the aisle screaming repeatedly, stopping halfway to look back. The Two Streetcleaners seize Lord Mulligan by either arm as he crumples.*]

Pack Lord Mulligan's body in dry ice! Ship Air Express to Cobh care of Mulligan Iron & Steel Works, in Cobh!

[*She runs sobbing out of the back of the auditorium as the whistle blows repeatedly and a Voice shouts.*]

I'm coming! I'm coming!

MARGUERITE:

Jacques! Jacques! Oh, God!

PILOT:

The Fugitivo is leaving, all aboard!

[*He starts toward the steps. Marguerite clutches his arm.*]

Let go of me!

MARGUERITE:

You can't go without me!

PILOT:

Officer, hold this woman!

JACQUES:

Marguerite, let him go!

[*She releases the Pilot's arm and turns savagely on Jacques. She tears his coat open, seizes a large envelope of papers and rushes after the Pilot who has started down the steps over the orchestra pit and into a center aisle of the house. Timpani build up as she starts down the steps, screaming—*]

MARGUERITE:

Here! I have them here! Wait! I have my papers now, I have my papers!

[*The Pilot runs cursing up the center aisle as the Fugitivo whistle gives repeated short, shrill blasts; timpani and dissonant brass are heard.*

[*Outgoing Passengers burst into hysterical song, laughter, shouts of farewell. These can come over a loudspeaker at the back of the house.*]

VOICE IN DISTANCE:

Going! Going! Going!

MARGUERITE [*attempting as if half paralyzed to descend the steps*]:

NOT WITHOUT ME, NO, NO, NOT WITHOUT ME!

[*Her figure is caught in the dazzling glacial light of the follow-spot. It blinds her. She makes violent, crazed gestures, clinging to the railing of the steps; her breath is loud and hoarse as a dying person's, she holds a bloodstained handkerchief to her lips.*

[*There is a prolonged, gradually fading, rocketlike roar as the Fugitivo takes off. Shrill cries of joy from departing passengers; something radiant passes above the stage and streams of confetti and tinsel fall into the plaza. Then there is a great calm, the ship's receding roar diminished to the hum of an insect.*]

GUTMAN [*somewhat compassionately*]:

Block Ten on the Camino Real.

There is something about the desolation of the plaza that suggests a city devastated by bombardment. Reddish lights flicker here and there as if ruins were smoldering and wisps of smoke rise from them.

LA MADRECITA [*almost inaudibly*]:
Donde?

THE DREAMER:
Aquí. Aquí, Madrecita.

MARGUERITE:
Lost! Lost! Lost! Lost!

[*She is still clinging brokenly to the railing of the steps. Jacques descends to her and helps her back up the steps.*]

JACQUES:
Lean against me, cara. Breathe quietly, now.

MARGUERITE:
Lost!

JACQUES:
Breathe quietly, quietly, and look up at the sky.

MARGUERITE:
Lost . . .

JACQUES:
These tropical nights are so clear. There's the Southern Cross. Do you see the Southern Cross, Marguerite?

[*He points through the proscenium. They are now on the bench before the fountain; she is resting in his arms.*]

And there, over there, is Orion, like a fat, golden fish swimming north in the deep clear water, and we are together, breathing quietly together, leaning together, quietly, quietly together, completely, sweetly together, not frightened, now, not alone, but completely·quietly together . . .

[*La Madrecita, led into the center of the plaza by her son, has begun to sing very softly; the reddish flares dim out and the smoke disappears.*]

All of us have a desperate bird in our hearts, a memory of— some distant mother with—wings . . .

MARGUERITE:
I would have—left—without you . . .

JACQUES:
I know, I know!

MARGUERITE:
Then how can you—still—?

JACQUES:
Hold you?

[*Marguerite nods slightly.*]

Because you've taught me that part of love which is tender. I never knew it before. Oh, I had—mistresses that circled me like moons! I scrambled from one bed chamber to another bed chamber with shirttails always aflame, from girl to girl, like buckets of coal oil poured on a conflagration! But never loved until now with the part of love that's tender . . .

MARGUERITE:
—We're used to each other. That's what you think is love . . . You'd better leave me now, you'd better go and let me go because there's a cold wind blowing out of the mountains and over the desert and into my heart, and if you stay with me now, I'll say cruel things, I'll wound your vanity, I'll taunt you with the decline of your male vigor!

JACQUES:

Why does disappointment make people unkind to each other?

MARGUERITE:

Each of us is very much alone.

JACQUES:

Only if we distrust each other.

MARGUERITE:

We have to distrust each other. It is our only defense against betrayal.

JACQUES:

I think our defense is love.

MARGUERITE:

Oh, Jacques, we're used to each other, we're a pair of captive hawks caught in the same cage, and so we've grown used to each other. That's what passes for love at this dim, shadowy end of the Camino Real ...

What are we sure of? Not even of our existence, dear comforting friend! And whom can we ask the questions that torment us? "What is this place?" "Where are we?"—a fat old man who gives sly hints that only bewilder us more, a fake of a Gypsy squinting at cards and tea leaves. What else are we offered? The never-broken procession of little events that assure us that we and strangers about us are still going on! Where? Why? and the perch that we hold is unstable! We're threatened with eviction, for this is a port of entry and departure, there are no permanent guests! And where else have we to go when we leave here? Bide-a-While? "Ritz Men Only"? Or under that ominous arch into Terra Incognita? We're lonely. We're frightened. We hear the Streetcleaners' piping not far away. So now and then, although we've wounded each other time and again—we stretch out hands to each other in the dark that we can't escape from—we huddle together for some dim-communal comfort—and that's what passes for love on this terminal stretch of the road that used to be royal. What is it, this feeling between us? When you feel my exhausted weight against your shoulder—when I clasp your anxious old hawk's head to my breast, what is it we feel in whatever is left of our hearts? Something, yes, something—delicate, unreal, bloodless! The sort of violets that could grow on the moon, or in the crevices of those far away mountains, fertilized by the droppings of carrion birds. Those birds are familiar to us. Their shadows inhabit the plaza. I've heard them flapping their wings like old charwomen beating worn-out carpets with gray brooms ...

But tenderness, the violets in the mountains—can't break the rocks!

JACQUES:
The violets in the mountains can break the rocks if you believe in them and allow them to grow!

[*The plaza has resumed its usual aspect. Abdullah enters through one of the downstage arches.*]

ABDULLAH:
Get your carnival hats and noisemakers here! Tonight the moon will restore the virginity of my sister!

MARGUERITE [*almost tenderly touching his face*]:
Don't you know that tonight I am going to betray you?

JACQUES:
—Why would you do that?

MARGUERITE:
Because I've outlived the tenderness of my heart. Abdullah,

97

come here! I have an errand for you! Go to Ahmed's and deliver a message!

ABDULLAH:

I'm working for Mama, making the Yankee dollar! Get your carnival hats and—

MARGUERITE:

Here, boy!

[*She snatches a ring off her finger and offers it to him.*]

JACQUES:

—Your cabochon sapphire?

MARGUERITE:

Yes, my cabochon sapphire!

JACQUES:

Are you mad?

MARGUERITE:

Yes, I'm mad, or nearly! The specter of lunacy's at my heels tonight!

[*Jacques drives Abdullah back with his cane.*]

Catch, boy! The other side of the fountain! Quick!

[*The guitar is heard molto vivace. She tosses the ring across the fountain. Jacques attempts to hold the boy back with his cane. Abdullah dodges in and out like a little terrier, laughing. Marguerite shouts encouragement in French. When the boy is driven back from the ring, she snatches it up and tosses it to him again, shouting:*]

Catch, boy! Run to Ahmed's! Tell the charming young man that the French lady's bored with her company tonight! Say that the French lady missed the Fugitivo and wants to forget

98

she missed it! Oh, and reserve a room with a balcony so I can watch your sister appear on the roof when the moonrise makes her a virgin!

[*Abdullah skips shouting out of the plaza. Jacques strikes the stage with his cane. She says, without looking at him:*]

Time betrays us and we betray each other.

JACQUES:
Wait, Marguerite.

MARGUERITE:
No! I can't! The wind from the desert is sweeping me away!

[*A loud singing wind sweeps her toward the terrace, away from him. She looks back once or twice as if for some gesture of leave-taking but he only stares at her fiercely, striking the stage at intervals with his cane, like a death march. Gutman watches, smiling, from the terrace, bows to Marguerite as she passes into the hotel. The drum of Jacques' cane is taken up by other percussive instruments, and almost unnoticeably at first, weird-looking celebrants or carnival mummers creep into the plaza, silently as spiders descending a wall.*]

[*A sheet of scarlet and yellow rice paper bearing some cryptic device is lowered from the center of the plaza. The percussive effects become gradually louder. Jacques is oblivious to the scene behind him, standing in front of the plaza, his eyes closed.*]

GUTMAN:
Block Eleven on the Camino Real.

BLOCK ELEVEN

GUTMAN:

The Fiesta has started. The first event is the coronation of the King of Cuckolds.

[*Blinding shafts of light are suddenly cast upon Casanova on the forestage. He shields his face, startled, as the crowd closes about him. The blinding shafts of light seem to strike him like savage blows and he falls to his knees as—*

[*The Hunchback scuttles out of the Gypsy's stall with a crown of gilded antlers on a velvet pillow. He places it on Jacques' head. The celebrants form a circle about him chanting.*]

JACQUES:

What is this?—a crown—

GUTMAN:

A crown of horns!

CROWD:

Cornudo! Cornudo! Cornudo! Cornudo! Cornudo!

GUTMAN:

Hail, all hail, the King of Cuckolds on the Camino Real!

[*Jacques springs up, first striking out at them with his cane. Then all at once he abandons self-defense, throws off his cape, casts away his cane, and fills the plaza with a roar of defiance and self-derision.*]

JACQUES:

Si, si, sono cornudo! Cornudo! Cornudo! Casanova is the King of Cuckolds on the Camino Real! Show me crowned to the world! Announce the honor! Tell the world of the honor bestowed on Casanova, Chevalier·de Seingalt! Knight

of the Golden Spur by the Grace of His Holiness the Pope
. . . Famous adventurer! Con man Extraordinary! Gambler!
Pitchman par excellence! Shill! Pimp! Spiv! *And—great—
lover* . . .

[*The Crowd howls with applause and laughter but his voice
rises above them with sobbing intensity.*]

Yes, I said GREAT LOVER! The greatest lover wears the
longest horns on the Camino! GREAT! LOVER!

GUTMAN:
Attention! Silence! The moon is rising! The restoration is
about to occur!

[*A white radiance is appearing over the ancient wall of the
town. The mountains become luminous. There is music.
Everyone, with breathless attention, faces the light.*

[*Kilroy crosses to Jacques and beckons him out behind the
crowd. There he snatches off the antlers and returns him his
fedora. Jacques reciprocates by removing Kilroy's fright
wig and electric nose. They embrace as brothers. In a Chap-
linesque dumb-play, Kilroy points to the wildly flickering
three brass balls of the Loan Shark and to his golden gloves:
then with a terrible grimace he removes the gloves from
about his neck, smiles at Jacques and indicates that the two
of them together will take flight over the wall. Jacques
shakes his head sadly, pointing to his heart and then to the
Siete Mares. Kilroy nods with regretful understanding of a
human and manly folly. A Guard has been silently approaching them in a soft-shoe dance. Jacques whistles "La
Golondrina." Kilroy assumes a very nonchalant pose. The
Guard picks up curiously the discarded fright wig and
electric nose. Then glancing suspiciously at the pair, he
advances. Kilroy makes a run for it. He does a baseball*

*slide into the Loan Shark's welcoming doorway. The door
slams. The Cop is about to crash it when a gong sounds
and Gutman shouts:*]

GUTMAN:

SILENCE! ATTENTION! THE GYPSY!

GYPSY [*appearing on the roof with a gong*]:
The moon has restored the virginity of my daughter Esmeralda!

[*The gong sounds.*]

STREET PEOPLE:
Ahh!

GYPSY:
The moon in its plenitude has made her a virgin!

[*The gong sounds.*]

STREET PEOPLE:
Ahh!

GYPSY:
Praise her, celebrate her, give her suitable homage!

[*The gong sounds.*]

STREET PEOPLE:
Ahh!

GYPSY:
Summon her to the roof!

[*She shouts:*]

ESMERALDA!

[*Dancers shout the name in rhythm.*]

RISE WITH THE MOON, MY DAUGHTER! CHOOSE THE HERO!

[*Esmeralda appears on the roof in dazzling light. She seems to be dressed in jewels. She raises her jeweled arms with a harsh flamenco cry.*]

ESMERALDA:
OLE!

DANCERS:
OLE!

[*The details of the Carnival are a problem for director and choreographer but it has already been indicated in the script that the Fiesta is a sort of serio-comic, grotesque-lyric "Rites of Fertility" with roots in various pagan cultures.*]

[*It should not be overelaborated or allowed to occupy much time. It should not be more than three minutes from the appearance of Esmeralda on the Gypsy's roof till the return of Kilroy from the Loan Shark's.*]

[*Kilroy emerges from the pawn shop in grotesque disguise, a turban, dark glasses, a burnoose and an umbrella or sunshade.*]

KILROY [*to Jacques*]:

So long, pal, I wish you could come with me.

[*Jacques clasps his cross in Kilroy's hands.*]

ESMERALDA:
Yankee!

KILROY [*to the audience*]:
So long, everybody. Good luck to you all on the Camino! I

103

hocked my golden gloves to finance this expedition. I'm going. Hasta luega. I'm going. I'm gone!

ESMERALDA:

Yankee!

[*He has no sooner entered the plaza than the riotous women strip off everything but the dungarees and skivvy which he first appeared in.*]

KILROY [*to the women*]:

Let me go. Let go of me! Watch out for my equipment!

ESMERALDA:

Yankee! Yankee!

[*He breaks away from them and plunges up the stairs of the ancient wall. He is halfway up them when Gutman shouts out:*]

GUTMAN:

Follow-spot on that gringo, light the stairs!

[*The light catches Kilroy. At the same instant Esmeralda cries out to him:*]

ESMERALDA:

Yankee! Yankee!

GYPSY:

What's goin' on down there?

[*She rushes into the plaza.*]

KILROY:

Oh, no, I'm on my way out!

ESMERALDA:

Espere un momento!

[*The Gypsy calls the police, but is ignored in the crowd.*]

KILROY:

Don't tempt me, baby! I hocked my golden gloves to finance this expedition!

ESMERALDA:

Querido!

KILROY:

Querido means sweetheart, a word which is hard to resist but I must resist it.

ESMERALDA:

Champ!

KILROY:

I used to be Champ but why remind me of it?

ESMERALDA:

Be Champ again! Contend in the contest! Compete in the competition!

GYPSY [*shouting*]:
Naw, naw, not eligible!

ESMERALDA:
Pl-eeeeeeze!

GYPSY:

Slap her, Nursie, she's flippin'.

[*Esmeralda slaps Nursie instead.*]

ESMERALDA:

Hero! Champ!

KILROY:

I'm not in condition!

105

ESMERALDA:

You're still the Champ, the undefeated Champ of the golden gloves!

KILROY:

Nobody's called me that in a long, long time!

ESMERALDA:

Champ!

KILROY:

My resistance is crumbling!

ESMERALDA:

Champ!

KILROY:

It's crumbled!

ESMERALDA:

Hero!

KILROY:

GERONIMO!

[*He takes a flying leap from the stairs into the center of the plaza. He turns toward Esmeralda and cries:*]

DOLL!!

[*Kilroy surrounded by cheering Street People goes into a triumphant eccentric dance which reviews his history as fighter, traveler and lover.*

[*At finish of the dance, the music is cut off, as Kilroy lunges, arm uplifted toward Esmeralda, and cries:*]

KILROY:

Kilroy the Champ!

ESMERALDA:

KILROY the Champ!

[*She snatches a bunch of red roses from the stunned Nursie and tosses them to Kilroy.*]

CROWD [*sharply*]:

OLE!

[*The Gypsy, at the same instant, hurls her gong down, creating a resounding noise.*

[*Kilroy turns and comes down toward the audience, saying to them:*]

KILROY:

Y'see?

[*Cheering Street People surge toward him and lift him in the air. The lights fade as the curtain descends.*]

CROWD [*in a sustained yell*]:

OLE!

[*The curtain falls. There is a short intermission.*]

BLOCK TWELVE

The stage is in darkness except for a spotlight which picks out Esmeralda on the Gypsy's roof.

ESMERALDA:

Mama, what happened? —Mama, the lights went out!— Mama, where are you? It's so dark I'm scared!—MAMA!

[*The lights are turned on displaying a deserted plaza. The Gypsy is seated at a small table before her stall.*]

GYPSY:

Come on downstairs, Doll. The mischief is done. You've chosen your hero!

GUTMAN [*from the balcony of the Siete Mares*]:
Block Twelve on the Camino Real.

NURSIE [*at the fountain*]:
Gypsy, the fountain is still dry!

GYPSY:

What d'yuh expect? There's nobody left to uphold the old traditions! You raise a girl. She watches television. Plays bebop. Reads *Screen Secrets*. Comes the Big Fiesta. The moonrise makes her a virgin—which is the neatest trick of the week! And what does she do? Chooses a Fugitive Patsy for the Chosen Hero! Well, show him in! Admit the joker and get the virgin ready!

NURSIE:

You're going through with it?

GYPSY:

Look, Nursie! I'm operating a legitimate joint! This joker'll get the same treatment he'd get if he breezed down the

Camino in a blizzard of G-notes! Trot, girl! Lubricate your means of locomotion!

[*Nursie goes into the Gypsy's stall. The Gypsy rubs her hands together and blows on the crystal ball, spits on it and gives it the old one-two with a "shammy" rag . . . She mutters "Crystal ball, tell me all . . . crystal ball tell me all" . . . as:*

[*Kilroy bounds into the plaza from her stall . . . a rose between his teeth.*]

GYPSY:
Siente se, por favor.

KILROY:
No comprendo the lingo.

GYPSY:
Put it down!

NURSIE [*offstage*]:
Hey, Gypsy!

GYPSY:
Address me as Madam!

NURSIE [*entering*]:
Madam! Winchell has scooped you!

GYPSY:
In a pig's eye!

NURSIE:
The Fugitivo has "*fftt . . .*"!

GYPSY:
In Elizabeth, New Jersey . . . ten fifty seven P.M. . . . Eastern Standard Time—while you were putting them kiss-me-quicks in your hair-do! Furthermore, my second exclusive is that the

109

solar system is drifting toward the constellation of Hercules: *Skiddoo!*

[*Nursie exits. Stamping is heard offstage.*]

Quiet, back there! God damn it!

NURSIE [*offstage*]:
She's out of control!

GYPSY:
Give her a double-bromide!

[*To Kilroy:*]

Well, how does it feel to be the Chosen Hero?

KILROY:
I better explain something to you.

GYPSY:
Save your breath. You'll need it.

KILROY:
I want to level with you. Can I level with you?

GYPSY [*rapidly stamping some papers*]:
How could you help but level with the Gypsy?

KILROY:
I don't know what the hero is chosen for

[*Esmeralda and Nursie shriek offstage.*]

GYPSY:
Time will brief you . . . Aw, I hate paper work! . . . NURS-EHH!

[*Nursie comes out and stands by the table.*]

This filing system is screwed up six ways from next Sunday . . . File this crap under crap!—

[*To Kilroy:*]

The smoking lamp is lit. Have a stick on me!

[*She offers him a cigarette.*]

KILROY:
No thanks.

GYPSY:
Come on, indulge yourself. You got nothing to lose that won't be lost.

KILROY:
If that's a professional opinion, I don't respect it.

GYPSY:
Resume your seat and give me your full name.

KILROY:
Kilroy.

GYPSY [*writing all this down*]:
Date of birth and place of that disaster?

KILROY:
Both unknown.

GYPSY:
Address?

KILROY:
Traveler.

GYPSY:
Parents?

KILROY:

Anonymous.

GYPSY:

Who brought you up?

KILROY:

I was brought up and down by an eccentric old aunt in Dallas.

GYPSY:

Raise both hands simultaneously and swear that you have not come here for the purpose of committing an immoral act.

ESMERALDA [*from offstage*]:

Hey, Chico!

GYPSY:

QUIET! Childhood diseases?

KILROY:

Whooping cough, measles and mumps.

GYPSY:

Likes and dislikes?

KILROY:

I like situations I can get out of. I don't like cops and—

GYPSY:

Immaterial! Here! Signature on this!

[*She hands him a blank.*]

KILROY:

What is it?

GYPSY:

You always sign something, don't you?

KILROY:
Not till I know what it is.

GYPSY:
It's just a little formality to give a tone to the establishment and make an impression on our out-of-town trade. Roll up your sleeve.

KILROY:
What for?

GYPSY:
A shot of some kind.

KILROY:
What kind?

GYPSY:
Any kind. Don't they always give you some kind of a shot?

KILROY:
"They"?

GYPSY:
Brass hats, Americanos!

[*She injects a hypo.*]

KILROY:
I am no guinea pig!

GYPSY:
Don't kid yourself. We're all of us guinea pigs in the laboratory of God. Humanity is just a work in progress.

KILROY:
I don't make it out.

GYPSY:

Who does? The Camino Real is a funny paper read backward!

[*There is weird piping outside. Kilroy shifts on his seat. The Gypsy grins.*]

Tired? The altitude makes you sleepy?

KILROY:

It makes me nervous.

GYPSY:

I'll show you how to take a slug of tequila! It dilates the capillaries. First you sprinkle salt on the back of your hand. Then lick it off with your tongue. Now then you toss the shot down!

[*She demonstrates.*]

—And then you bite into the lemon. That way it goes down easy, but what a bang! —You're next.

KILROY:

No, thanks, I'm on the wagon.

GYPSY:

There's an old Chinese proverb that says, "When your goose is cooked you might as well have it cooked with plenty of gravy."

[*She laughs.*]

Get up, baby. Let's have a look at yuh!—You're not a bad-looking boy. Sometimes working for the Yankee dollar isn't a painful profession. Have you ever been attracted by older women?

KILROY:

Frankly, no, ma'am.

GYPSY:

Well, there's a first time for everything.

KILROY:

That is a subject I cannot agree with you on.

GYPSY:

You think I'm an old bag?

[*Kilroy laughs awkwardly. The Gypsy slaps his face.*]

Will you take the cards or the crystal?

KILROY:

It's immaterial.

GYPSY:

All right, we'll begin with the cards.

[*She shuffles and deals.*]

Ask me a question.

KILROY:

Has my luck run out?

GYPSY:

Baby, your luck ran out the day you were born. Another question.

KILROY:

Ought I to leave this town?

GYPSY:

It don't look to me like you've got much choice in the matter ... Take a card.

115

[*Kilroy takes one.*]

GYPSY:
Ace?

KILROY:
Yes, ma'am.

GYPSY:
What color?

KILROY:
Black.

GYPSY:
Oh, oh—That does it. How big is your heart?

KILROY:
As big as the head of a baby.

GYPSY:
It's going to **break**.

KILROY:
That's what I was afraid of.

GYPSY:
The Streetcleaners are waiting for you outside the door.

KILROY:
Which door, the front one? I'll slip out the back!

GYPSY:
Leave us face it frankly, your number is up! You must've known a long time that the name of Kilroy was on the Streetcleaners' list.

KILROY:
Sure. But not on top of it!

GYPSY:

It's always a bit of a shock. Wait a minute! Here's good news. The Queen of Hearts has turned up in proper position.

KILROY:

What's that mean?

GYPSY:

Love, baby!

KILROY:

Love?

GYPSY:

The Booby Prize! —Esmeralda!

[*She rises and hits a gong. A divan is carried out. The Gypsy's Daughter is seated in a reclining position, like an odalisque, on this low divan. A spangled veil covers her face. From this veil to the girdle below her navel, that supports her diaphanous bifurcated skirt, she is nude except for a pair of glittering emerald snakes coiled over her breasts. Kilroy's head moves in a dizzy circle and a canary warbles inside it.*]

KILROY:

WHAT'S—WHAT'S *HER* SPECIALTY?—Tea leaves?

[*The Gypsy wags a finger.*]

GYPSY:

You know what curiosity did to the tomcat!—Nursie, give me my glamor wig and my forty-five. I'm hitting the street! I gotta go down to Walgreen's for change.

KILROY:

What change?

GYPSY:

The change from that ten-spot you're about to give me.

NURSIE:

Don't argue with her. She has a will of iron.

KILROY:

I'm not arguing!

[*He reluctantly produces the money.*]

But let's be *fair* about this! I hocked my golden gloves for this sawbuck!

NURSIE:

All of them Yankee bastids want something for nothing!

KILROY:

I want a receipt for this bill.

NURSIE:

No one is gypped at the Gypsy's!

KILROY:

That's wonderful! How do I know it?

GYPSY:

It's in the cards, it's in the crystal ball, it's in the tea leaves! Absolutely no one is gypped at the Gypsy's!

[*She snatches the bill. The wind howls.*]

Such changeable weather! I'll slip on my summer furs! Nursie, break out my summer furs!

NURSIE [*leering grotesquely*]:
Mink or sable?

GYPSY:
Ha ha, that's a doll! Here! Clock him!

118

[*Nursie tosses her a greasy blanket, and the Gypsy tosses Nursie an alarm clock. The Gypsy rushes through the beaded string curtains.*]

Adios! Ha ha!!

[*She is hardly offstage when two shots ring out. Kilroy starts.*]

ESMERALDA [*plaintively*]:
Mother has such an awful time on the street.

KILROY:
You mean that she is insulted on the street?

ESMERALDA:
By strangers.

KILROY [*to the audience*]:
I shouldn't think acquaintances would do it.

[*She curls up on the low divan. Kilroy licks his lips.*]

—You seem very different from—this afternoon . . .

ESMERALDA:
This afternoon?

KILROY:
Yes, in the plaza when I was being roughed up by them gorillas and you was being dragged in the house by your Mama!

[*Esmeralda stares at him blankly.*]

You don't remember?

ESMERALDA:
I never remember what happened before the moonrise makes me a virgin.

KILROY:
—That—comes as a shock to you, huh?

ESMERALDA:
Yes. It comes as a shock.

KILROY [*smiling*]:
You have a little temporary amnesia they call it!

ESMERALDA:
Yankee . . .

KILROY:
Huh?

ESMERALDA:
I'm glad I chose you. I'm glad that you were chosen.

[*Her voice trails off.*]

I'm glad. I'm very glad . . .

NURSIE:
Doll!

ESMERALDA:
—What is it, Nursie?

NURSIE:
How are things progressing?

ESMERALDA:
Slowly, Nursie—

[*Nursie comes lumbering in.*]

NURSIE:
I want some light reading matter.

ESMERALDA:

He's sitting on *Screen Secrets*.

KILROY [*jumping up*]:

Aw. Here.

[*He hands her the fan magazine. She lumbers back out, coyly.*]

—I—I feel——self-conscious . .

[*He suddenly jerks out a silver-framed photo.*]

—D'you—like pictures?

ESMERALDA:

Moving pictures?

KILROY:

No, a—motionless—snapshot!

ESMERALDA:

Of you?

KILROY:

Of my—real—true woman . . . She was a platinum blonde the same as Jean Harlow. Do you remember Jean Harlow? No, you wouldn't remember Jean Harlow. It shows you are getting old when you remember Jean Harlow.

[*He puts the snapshot away.*]

. . . They say that Jean Harlow's ashes are kept in a little private cathedral in Forest Lawn . . . Wouldn't it be wonderful if you could sprinkle them ashes over the ground like seeds, and out of each one would spring another Jean Harlow? And when spring comes you could just walk out and pick them off the bush! . . . You don't talk much.

121

ESMERALDA:

You want me to *talk*?

KILROY:

Well, that's the way we do things in the States. A little vino, some records on the Victrola, some quiet conversation—and then if both parties are in a mood for romance . . . Romance—

ESMERALDA:

Music!

[*She rises and pours some wine from a slender crystal decanter as music is heard.*]

They say that the monetary system has got to be stabilized all over the world.

KILROY [*taking the glass*]:

Repeat that, please. My radar was not wide open.

ESMERALDA:

I said that *they* said that—uh, skip it! But we couldn't care less as long as we keep on getting the Yankee dollar . . . plus federal tax!

KILROY:

That's for surely!

ESMERALDA:

How do you feel about the class struggle? Do you take sides in that?

KILROY:

Not that I—

ESMERALDA:

Neither do we because of the dialectics.

KILROY:

Who! Which?

ESMERALDA:

Languages with accents, I suppose. But Mama don't care as long as they don't bring the Pope over here and put him in the White House.

KILROY:

Who would do that?

ESMERALDA:

Oh, the Bolsheviskies, those nasty old things with whiskers! *Whiskers scratch!* But little moustaches tickle ...

[*She giggles.*]

KILROY:

I always got a smooth shave ...

ESMERALDA:

And how do you feel about the Mumbo Jumbo? Do you think they've got the Old Man in the bag yet?

KILROY:

The Old Man?

ESMERALDA:

God. We don't think so. We think there has been so much of the Mumbo Jumbo it's put Him to sleep!

[*Kilroy jumps up impatiently.*]

KILROY:

This is not what I mean by a quiet conversation. I mean this is no where! *No where!*

ESMERALDA:

What sort of talk do you want?

123

KILROY:

Something more—intimate sort of! You know, like—

ESMERALDA:

—Where did you get those eyes?

KILROY:

PERSONAL! Yeah ...

ESMERALDA:

Well,—where did you get those eyes?

KILROY:

Out of a dead codfish!

NURSIE [*shouting offstage*]:

DOLL!

[*Kilroy springs up, pounding his left palm with his right fist.*]

ESMERALDA:

What?

NURSIE:

Fifteen minutes!

KILROY:

I'm no hot-rod mechanic.

[*To the audience:*]

I bet she's out there holding a stop watch to see that I don't overstay my time in this place!

ESMERALDA [*calling through the string curtains*]:

Nursie, go to bed, Nursie!

KILROY [*in a fierce whisper*]:

That's right, go to bed, Nursie!!

[*There is a loud crash offstage.*]

ESMERALDA:
—Nursie has gone to bed . . .

[*She drops the string curtains and returns to the alcove.*]

KILROY [*with vast relief*]:
—Ahhhhhhhhhh . . .

ESMERALDA:
What've you got your eyes on?

KILROY:
Those green snakes on you—what do you wear them for?

ESMERALDA:
Supposedly for protection, but really for fun.

[*He crosses to the divan.*]

What are you going to do?

KILROY:
I'm about to establish a beachhead on that sofa.

[*He sits down.*]

How about—lifting your veil?

ESMERALDA:
I can't lift it.

KILROY:
Why not?

ESMERALDA:
I promised Mother I wouldn't.

KILROY:
I thought your mother was the broad-minded type.

125

ESMERALDA:

Oh, she is, but you know how mothers are. You can lift it for me, if you say pretty please.

KILROY:

Aww——

ESMERALDA:

Go on, say it! Say pretty please!

KILROY:

No!!

ESMERALDA:

Why not?

KILROY:

It's silly.

ESMERALDA:

Then you can't lift my veil!

KILROY:

Oh, all right. Pretty please.

ESMERALDA:

Say it again!

KILROY:

Pretty please.

ESMERALDA:

Now say it once more like you meant it.

[*He jumps up. She grabs his hand.*]

Don't go away.

KILROY:

You're making a fool out of me.

ESMERALDA:

I was just teasing a little. Because you're so cute. Sit down again, please—*pretty* please!

[*He falls on the couch.*]

KILROY:

What is that wonderful perfume you've got on?

ESMERALDA:

Guess!

KILROY:

Chanel Number Five?

ESMERALDA:

No.

KILROY:

Tabu?

ESMERALDA:

No.

KILROY:

I give up.

ESMERALDA:

It's *Noche en Acapulco*! I'm just dying to go to Acapulco. I wish that you would take me to Acapulco.

[*He sits up.*]

What's the matter?

KILROY:

You Gypsies' daughters are invariably reminded of something without which you cannot do—just when it looks like everything has been fixed.

127

ESMERALDA:

That isn't nice at all. I'm not the gold-digger type. Some girls see themselves in silver foxes. I only see myself in Acapulco!

KILROY:

At Todd's Place?

ESMERALDA:

Oh, no, at the Mirador! Watching those pretty boys dive off the Quebrada!

KILROY:

Look again, baby. Maybe you'll see yourself in Paramount Pictures or having a Singapore Sling at a Statler bar!

ESMERALDA:

You're being sarcastic?

KILROY:

Nope. Just realistic. All of you Gypsies' daughters have hearts of stone, and I'm not whistling "Dixie"! But just the same, the night before a man dies, he says, "Pretty please—will you let me lift your veil?"—while the Streetcleaners wait for him right outside the door!—Because to be warm for a little longer is life. And love?—that's a four-letter word which is sometimes no better than one you see printed on fences by kids playing hooky from school!—Oh, well—what's the use of complaining? You Gypsies' daughters have ears that only catch sounds like the snap of a gold cigarette case! Or, pretty please, baby,—we're going to Acapulco!

ESMERALDA:

Are we?

KILROY:

See what I mean?

[*To the audience:*]

Didn't I tell you?!

[*To Esmeralda:*]

Yes! In the morning!

ESMERALDA:
Ohhhh! I'm dizzy with joy! My little heart is going pitty-pat!

KILROY:
My big heart is going boom-boom! Can I lift your veil now?

ESMERALDA:
If you will be gentle.

KILROY:
I would not hurt a fly unless it had on leather mittens.

[*He touches a corner of her spangled veil.*]

ESMERALDA:
Ohhh ...

KILROY:
What?

ESMERALDA:
Ohhhhhh!!

KILROY:
Why! What's the matter?

ESMERALDA:
You are not being gentle!

KILROY:
I *am* being gentle.

129

ESMERALDA:

You are *not* being gentle.

KILROY:

What was I being, then?

ESMERALDA:

Rough!

KILROY:

I am *not* being rough.

ESMERALDA:

Yes, you *are* being rough. You have to be gentle with me because you're the first.

KILROY:

Are you kidding?

ESMERALDA:

No.

KILROY:

How about all of those other fiestas you've been to?

ESMERALDA:

Each one's the first one. That is the wonderful thing about Gypsies' daughters!

KILROY:

You can say that again!

ESMERALDA:

I don't like you when you're like that.

KILROY:

Like what?

ESMERALDA:

Cynical and sarcastic.

KILROY:

I am sincere.

ESMERALDA:

Lots of boys aren't sincere.

KILROY:

Maybe they aren't but I am.

ESMERALDA:

Everyone says he's sincere, but everyone isn't sincere. If everyone was sincere who says he's sincere there wouldn't be half so many insincere ones in the world and there would be lots, lots, lots more really sincere ones!

KILROY:

I think you have got something there. But how about Gypsies' daughters?

ESMERALDA:

Huh?

KILROY:

Are they one hundred per cent in the really sincere category?

ESMERALDA:

Well, yes, and no, mostly no! But some of them are for a while if their sweethearts are gentle.

KILROY:

Would you believe I am sincere and gentle?

ESMERALDA:

I would believe that you believe that you are . . . For a while . . .

KILROY:

Everything's for a while. For a while is the stuff that dreams are made of, Baby! Now?—Now?

ESMERALDA:

Yes, now, but be gentle!—*gentle* ...

[*He delicately lifts a corner of her veil. She utters a soft cry. He lifts it further. She cries out again. A bit further ... He turns the spangled veil all the way up from her face.*]

KILROY:

I am sincere.

ESMERALDA:

I am sincere.

KILROY:

I am sincere.

ESMERALDA:

I am sincere.

KILROY:

I am sincere.

ESMERALDA:

I am sincere.

KILROY:

I am sincere.

ESMERALDA:

I am sincere.

[*Kilroy leans back, removing his hand from her veil. She opens her eyes.*]

Is that all?

KILROY:

I am tired.

ESMERALDA:

—Already?

[*He rises and goes down the steps from the alcove.*]

KILROY:

I am tired, and full of regret ...

ESMERALDA:

Oh!

KILROY:

It wasn't much to give my golden gloves for.

ESMERALDA:

You pity yourself?

KILROY:

That's right, I pity myself and everybody that goes to the Gypsy's daughter. I pity the world and I pity the God who made it.

[*He sits down.*]

ESMERALDA:

It's always like that as soon as the veil is lifted. They're all so ashamed of having degraded themselves, and their hearts have more regret than a heart can hold!

KILROY:

Even a heart that's as big as the head of a baby!

ESMERALDA:

You don't even notice how pretty my face is, do you?

KILROY:

You look like all Gypsies' daughters, no better, no worse. But

133

as long as you get to go to Acapulco, your cup runneth over with ordinary contentment.

ESMERALDA:

—I've never been so insulted in all my life!

KILROY:

Oh, yes, you have, baby. And you'll be insulted worse if you stay in this racket. You'll be insulted so much that it will get to be like water off *a duck's back!*

[*The door slams. Curtains are drawn apart on the Gypsy. Esmeralda lowers her veil hastily. Kilroy pretends not to notice the Gypsy's entrance. She picks up a little bell and rings it over his head.*]

Okay, Mamacita! I am aware of your presence!

GYPSY:

Ha-ha! I was followed three blocks by some awful man!

KILROY:

Then you caught him.

GYPSY:

Naw, he ducked into a subway! I waited fifteen minutes outside the men's room and he never came out!

KILROY:

Then you went in?

GYPSY:

No! I got myself a sailor!—The streets are brilliant! . . . Have you all been good children?

[*Esmeralda makes a whimpering sound.*]

The pussy will play while the old mother cat is away?

134

KILROY:

Your sense of humor is wonderful, but how about my change, Mamacita?

GYPSY:

What change are you talking about?

KILROY:

Are you boxed out of your mind? The change from that ten-spot you trotted over to Walgreen's?

GYPSY:
Ohhhhh—

KILROY:
Oh, what?

GYPSY [*counting on her fingers*]:
Five for the works, one dollar luxury tax, two for the house percentage and two more pour la service!—makes ten! Didn't I tell you?

KILROY:
—What kind of a deal is this?

GYPSY [*whipping out a revolver*]:
A rugged one, Baby!

ESMERALDA:
Mama, don't be unkind!

GYPSY:
Honey, the gentleman's friends are waiting outside the door and it wouldn't be nice to detain him! Come on—Get going—Vamoose!

KILROY:
Okay, Mamacita! Me voy!

[*He crosses to the beaded string curtains, turns to look back at the Gypsy and her daughter. The piping of the Street-cleaners is heard outside.*]

Sincere?—Sure! That's the wonderful thing about Gypsies' daughters!

[*He goes out. Esmeralda raises a wondering fingertip to one eye. Then she cries out:*]

ESMERALDA:
Look, Mama! Look, Mama! A tear!

GYPSY:
You have been watching television too much . . .

[*She gathers the cards and turns off the crystal ball as—*

[*Light fades out on the phony paradise of the Gypsy's.*]

GUTMAN:
Block Thirteen on the Camino Real.

[*He exits.*]

BLOCK THIRTEEN

In the blackout the Streetcleaners place a barrel in the center and then hide in the Pit.

Kilroy, who enters from the right, is followed by a spotlight. He sees the barrel and the menacing Streetcleaners and then runs to the closed door of the Siete Mares and rings the bell. No one answers. He backs up so he can see the balcony and calls:

KILROY:

Mr. Gutman! Just gimme a cot in the lobby. I'll do odd jobs in the morning. I'll be the Patsy again. I'll light my nose sixty times a minute. I'll take pratfalls and assume the position for anybody that drops a dime on the street . . . Have a heart! Have just a LITTLE heart. Please!

[*There is no response from Gutman's balcony. Jacques enters. He pounds his cane once on the pavement.*]

JACQUES:

Gutman! Open the door!—*GUTMAN! GUTMAN!*

[*Eva, a beautiful woman, apparently nude, appears on the balcony.*]

GUTMAN [*from inside*]:

Eva darling, you're exposing yourself!

[*He appears on the balcony with a portmanteau.*]

JACQUES:

What are you doing with my portmanteau?

GUTMAN:

Haven't you come for your luggage?

137

JACQUES:
Certainly not! I haven't checked out of here!

GUTMAN:
Very few do . . . but residences are frequently terminated.

JACQUES:
Open the door!

GUTMAN:
Open the letter with the remittance check in it!

JACQUES:
In the morning!

GUTMAN:
Tonight!

JACQUES:
Upstairs in my room!

GUTMAN:
Downstairs at the entrance!

JACQUES:
I won't be intimidated!

GUTMAN [*raising the portmanteau over his head*]:
What?!

JACQUES:
Wait!—

[*He takes the letter out of his pocket.*]

Give me some light.

[*Kilroy strikes a match and holds it over Jacques' shoulder.*]

Thank you. What does it say?

GUTMAN:
—Remittances?

KILROY [*reading the letter over Jacques' shoulder*]:
—discontinued . . .

[*Gutman raises the portmanteau again.*]

JACQUES:
Careful, I have—

[*The portmanteau lands with a crash.*

[*The Bum comes to the window at the crash. A. Ratt comes out to his doorway at the same time.*]

—fragile—mementos . . .

[*He crosses slowly down to the portmanteau and kneels as . . .*

[*Gutman laughs and slams the balcony door. Jacques turns to Kilroy. He smiles at the young adventurer.*]

—"And so at last it has come, the distinguished thing!"

[*A. Ratt speaks as Jacques touches the portmanteau.*]

A. RATT
Hey, Dad—Vacancy here! A bed at the "Ritz Men Only." A little white ship to sail the dangerous night in.

JACQUES:
Single or double?

A. RATT
There's only singles in this pad.

JACQUES [*to Kilroy*]:
Match you for it.

KILROY:

What the hell, we're buddies, we can sleep spoons! If we can't sleep, we'll push the washstand against the door and sing old popular songs till the crack of dawn! . . . "Heart of my heart, I love that melody!" . . . You bet your life I do.

[*Jacques takes out a pocket handkerchief and starts to grasp the portmanteau handle.*]

—It looks to me like you could use a redcap and my rates are nonunion!

[*He picks up the portmanteau and starts to cross toward the "Ritz Men Only." He stops at right center.*]

Sorry, buddy. Can't make it! The altitude on this block has affected my ticker! And in the distance which is nearer than further, I hear—the Streetcleaners'—piping!

[*Piping is heard.*]

JACQUES:
COME ALONG!

[*He lifts the portmanteau and starts on.*]

KILROY:
NO. Tonight! I prefer! To sleep! Out! Under! The stars!

JACQUES [*gently*]:
I understand, Brother!

KILROY [*to Jacques as he continues toward the "Ritz Men Only"*]:

Bon Voyage! I hope that you sail the dangerous night to the sweet golden port of morning!

JACQUES [*exiting*]:
Thanks, Brother!

KILROY:
Excuse the *corn!* I'm sincere!

BUM:
Show me the way to go home! . . .

GUTMAN [*appearing on the balcony with white parakeet*]:
Block Fourteen on the Camino Real.

BLOCK FOURTEEN

At opening, the Bum is still at the window.

The Streetcleaners' piping continues a little louder. Kilroy climbs, breathing heavily, to the top of the stairs and stands looking out at Terra Incognita as . . .

Marguerite enters the plaza through alleyway at right. She is accompanied by a silent Young Man who wears a domino.

MARGUERITE:

Don't come any further with me. I'll have to wake the night porter. Thank you for giving me safe conduct through the Medina.

[*She has offered her hand. He grips it with a tightness that makes her wince.*]

Ohhhh . . . I'm not sure which is more provocative in you, your ominous silence or your glittering smile or—

[*He's looking at her purse.*]

What do you want? . . . Oh!

[*She starts to open the purse. He snatches it. She gasps as he suddenly strips her cloak off her. Then he snatches off her pearl necklace. With each successive despoilment, she gasps and retreats but makes no resistance. Her eyes are closed. He continues to smile. Finally, he rips her dress and runs his hands over her body as if to see if she had anything else of value concealed on her.*]

—What else do I have that you want?

THE YOUNG MAN [*contemptuously*]:
Nothing.

[*The Young Man exits through the cantina, examining his loot. The Bum leans out his window, draws a deep breath and says:*]

BUM:
Lonely.

MARGUERITE [*to herself*]:
Lonely . . .

KILROY [*on the steps*]:
Lonely . . .

[*The Streetcleaners' piping is heard.*]

[*Marguerite runs to the Siete Mares and rings the bell. Nobody answers. She crosses to the terrace. Kilroy, meanwhile, has descended the stairs.*]

MARGUERITE:
Jacques!

[*Piping is heard.*]

KILROY:
Lady?

MARGUERITE:
What?

KILROY:
—I'm—safe . . .

MARGUERITE:
I wasn't expecting that music tonight, were you?

[*Piping.*]

KILROY:
It's them Streetcleaners.

MARGUERITE:
I know.

[*Piping.*]

KILROY:
You better go on in, lady.

MARGUERITE:
No.

KILROY:
GO ON IN!

MARGUERITE:
NO! I want to stay out here and I do what I want to do!

[*Kilroy looks at her for the first time.*]

Sit down with me please.

KILROY:
They're coming for me. The Gypsy told me I'm on top of their list. Thanks for. Taking my. Hand.

[*Piping is heard.*]

MARGUERITE:
Thanks for taking mine.

[*Piping.*]

KILROY:
Do me one more favor. Take out of my pocket a picture. My fingers are. Stiff.

MARGUERITE:
This one?

144

KILROY:

My one. True. Woman.

MARGUERITE:

A silver-framed photo! Was she really so fair?

KILROY:

She was so fair and much fairer than they could tint that picture!

MARGUERITE:

Then you have been on the street when the street was royal.

KILROY:

Yeah . . . when the street was royal!

[*Piping is heard. Kilroy rises.*]

MARGUERITE:

Don't get up, don't leave me!

KILROY:

I want to be on my feet when the Streetcleaners come for me!

MARGUERITE:

Sit back down again and tell me about your girl.

[*He sits.*]

KILROY:

Y'know what it is you miss most? When you're separated. From someone. You lived. With. And loved? It's waking up in the night! With that—warmness beside you!

MARGUERITE:

Yes, that *warmness* beside you!

KILROY:

Once you get used to that. *Warmness!* It's a hell of a lonely feeling to wake up without it! Specially in some dollar-a-night hotel room on Skid! A hot-water bottle won't do. And a stranger. Won't do. It has to be some one you're used to. And that you. *KNOW LOVES* you!

[*Piping is heard.*]

Can you see them?

MARGUERITE:
I see no one but you.

KILROY:
I looked at my wife one night when she was sleeping and that was the night that the medics wouldn't okay me for no more fights . . . Well . . . My wife was sleeping with a smile like a child's. I kissed her. She didn't wake up. I took a pencil and paper. I wrote her. Good-bye!

MARGUERITE:
That was the night she would have loved you the most!

KILROY:
Yeah, *that* night, but what about *after* that night? Oh, lady . . . Why should a beautiful girl tie up with a broken-down champ?—The earth still turning and her obliged to turn with it, not out—of dark into light but out of light into dark? Naw, naw, naw, naw!—Washed up!—Finished!

[*Piping.*]

. . . that ain't a word that a man can't look at . . . There ain't no words in the language a man can't look at . . . and know just what they mean. And be. And act. And *go!*

[*He turns to the waiting Streetcleaners.*]

Come on! . . . Come on! . . . COME ON, YOU SONS OF BITCHES! KILROY IS HERE! HE'S READY!

[*A gong sounds.*

[*Kilroy swings at the Streetcleaners. They circle about him out of reach, turning him by each of their movements. The swings grow wilder like a boxer. He falls to his knees still swinging and finally collapses flat on his face.*

[*The Streetcleaners pounce but La Madrecita throws herself protectingly over the body and covers it with her shawl.*

[*Blackout.*]

MARGUERITE:
Jacques!

GUTMAN [*on balcony*]:
Block Fifteen on the Camino Real.

147

BLOCK FIFTEEN

*La Madrecita is seated; across her knees is the body of Kilroy.
Up center, a low table on wheels bears a sheeted figure. Beside
the table stands a Medical Instructor addressing Students and
Nurses, all in white surgical outfits.*

INSTRUCTOR:

This is the body of an unidentified vagrant.

LA MADRECITA:

This was thy son, America—and now mine.

INSTRUCTOR:

He was found in an alley along the Camino Real.

LA MADRECITA:

Think of him, now, as he was before his luck failed him.
Remember his time of greatness, when he was not faded, not
frightened.

INSTRUCTOR:

More light, please!

LA MADRECITA:

More light!

INSTRUCTOR:

Can everyone see clearly!

LA MADRECITA:

Everyone must see clearly!

INSTRUCTOR:

There is no external evidence of disease.

LA MADRECITA:

He had clear eyes and the body of a champion boxer.

148

INSTRUCTOR:

There are no marks of violence on the body.

LA MADRECITA:

He had the soft voice of the South and a pair of golden gloves.

INSTRUCTOR:

His death was apparently due to natural causes.

[*The Students make notes. There are keening voices.*]

LA MADRECITA:

Yes, blow wind where night thins! He had many admirers!

INSTRUCTOR:

There are no legal claimants.

LA MADRECITA:

He stood as a planet among the moons of their longing, haughty with youth, a champion of the prize-ring!

INSTRUCTOR:

No friends or relatives having identified him—

LA MADRECITA:

You should have seen the lovely monogrammed robe in which he strode the aisles of the colosseums!

INSTRUCTOR:

After the elapse of a certain number of days, his body becomes the property of the State—

LA MADRECITA:

Yes, blow wind where night thins—for laurel is not ever-lasting . . .

INSTRUCTOR:

And now is transferred to our hands for the nominal sum of five dollars.

LA MADRECITA:

This was thy son,—and now mine . . .

INSTRUCTOR:

We will now proceed with the dissection. Knife, please!

LA MADRECITA:

Blow wind!

[*Keening is heard offstage.*]

Yes, blow wind where night thins! You are his passing bell and his lamentation.

[*More keening is heard.*]

Keen for him, all maimed creatures, deformed and mutilated —his homeless ghost is your own!

INSTRUCTOR:

First we will open up the chest cavity and examine the heart for evidence of coronary occlusion.

LA MADRECITA:

His heart was pure gold and as big as the head of a baby.

INSTRUCTOR:

We will make an incision along the vertical line.

LA MADRECITA:

Rise, ghost! Go! Go bird! "Humankind cannot bear very much reality."

[*At the touch of her flowers, Kilroy stirs and pushes himself up slowly from her lap. On his feet again, he rubs his eyes and looks around him.*]

VOICES [*crying offstage*]:
Olé! Olé! Olé!

150

KILROY:

Hey! Hey, somebody! Where am I?

[*He notices the dissection room and approaches.*]

INSTRUCTOR [*removing a glittering sphere from a dummy corpse*]:

Look at this heart. It's as big as the head of a baby.

KILROY:

My heart!

INSTRUCTOR:

Wash it off so we can look for the pathological lesions.

KILROY:

Yes, siree, that's my heart!

GUTMAN:

Block Sixteen!

[*Kilroy pauses just outside the dissection area as a Student takes the heart and dips it into a basin on the stand beside the table. The Student suddenly cries out and holds aloft a glittering gold sphere.*]

INSTRUCTOR:

Look! This heart's solid gold!

BLOCK SIXTEEN

KILROY [*rushing forward*]:
That's mine, you bastards!

[*He snatches the golden sphere from the Medical Instructor. The autopsy proceeds as if nothing had happened as the spot of light on the table fades out, but for Kilroy a ghostly chase commences, a dreamlike re-enactment of the chase that occurred at the end of Block Six. Gutman shouts from his balcony:*]

GUTMAN:
Stop, thief, stop, corpse! That gold heart is the property of the State! Catch him, catch the golden-heart robber!

[*Kilroy dashes offstage into an aisle of the theatre. There is the wail of a siren: the air is filled with calls and whistles, roar of motors, screeching brakes, pistol-shots, thundering footsteps. The dimness of the auditorium is transected by searching rays of light—but there are no visible pursuers.*]

KILROY [*as he runs panting up the aisle*]:
This is my heart! It don't belong to no State, not even the U.S.A. Which way is out? Where's the Greyhound depot? Nobody's going to put my heart in a bottle in a museum and charge admission to support the rotten police! Where are they? Which way are they going? Or coming? Hey, somebody, help me get out of here! Which way do I—which way —which way do I—*go! go! go! go! go!*

[*He has now arrived in the balcony.*]

Gee, I'm lost! I don't know where I am! I'm all turned around, I'm *confused,* I don't understand—what's—happened, it's like a—*dream,* it's—just like a—dream . . . *Mary! Oh, Mary! Mary!*

[*He has entered the box from which he leapt in Block Two.*

[*A clear shaft of light falls on him. He looks up into it, crying:*]

Mary, help a Christian!! Help a Christian, Mary!—It's like a dream . . .

[*Esmeralda appears in a childish nightgown beside her gauze-tented bed on the Gypsy's roof. Her Mother appears with a cup of some sedative drink, cooing . . .*]

GYPSY:
Beddy-bye, beddy-bye, darling. It's sleepy-time down South and up North, too, and also East and West!

KILROY [*softly*]:
Yes, it's—like a—*dream* . . .

[*He leans panting over the ledge of the box, holding his heart like a football, watching Esmeralda.*]

GYPSY:
Drink your Ovaltine, Ducks, and the sandman will come on tiptoe with a bag full of dreams . . .

ESMERALDA:
I want to dream of the Chosen Hero, Mummy.

GYPSY:
Which one, the one that's coming or the one that is gone?

ESMERALDA:
The *only* one, *Kilroy*! He was *sincere*!

KILROY:
That's *right*! *I was*, for a while!

153

GYPSY:

How do you know that Kilroy was sincere?

ESMERALDA:

He said so.

KILROY:

That's the truth, I *was*!

GYPSY:

When did he say that?

ESMERALDA:

When he lifted my veil.

GYPSY:

Baby, they're always sincere when they lift your veil; it's one of those natural reflexes that don't mean a thing.

KILROY [*aside*]:

What a cynical old bitch that Gypsy mama is!

GYPSY:

And there's going to be lots of other fiestas for you, baby doll, and lots of other chosen heroes to lift your little veil when Mamacita and Nursie are out of the room.

ESMERALDA:

No, Mummy, never, I mean it!

KILROY:

I *believe* she means it!

GYPSY:

Finish your Ovaltine and say your Now-I-Lay-Me.

[*Esmeralda sips the drink and hands her the cup.*]

KILROY [*with a catch in his voice*]:
I had one true woman, which I can't go back to, but now I've found another.

[*He leaps onto the stage from the box.*]

ESMERALDA [*dropping to her knees*]:
Now I lay me down to sleep, I pray the Lord my soul to keep. If I should die before I wake, I pray the Lord my soul to take.

GYPSY:
God bless Mummy!

ESMERALDA:
And the crystal ball and the tea leaves.

KILROY:
Pssst!

ESMERALDA:
What's that?

GYPSY:
A tomcat in the plaza.

ESMERALDA:
God bless all cats without pads in the plaza tonight.

KILROY:
Amen!

[*He falls to his knees in the empty plaza.*]

ESMERALDA:
God bless all con men and hustlers and pitch-men who hawk their hearts on the street, all two-time losers who're likely to lose once more, the courtesan who made the mistake of love, the greatest of lovers crowned with the longest horns, the poet who wandered far from his heart's green country and possibly

will and possibly won't be able to find his way back, look down with a smile tonight on the last cavaliers, the ones with the rusty armor and soiled white plumes, and visit with understanding and something that's almost tender those fading legends that come and go in this plaza like songs not clearly remembered, oh, sometime and somewhere, let there be something to mean the word *honor* again!

QUIXOTE [*hoarsely and loudly, stirring slightly among his verminous rags*]:
Amen!

KILROY:
Amen . . .

GYPSY [*disturbed*]:
—That will do, now.

ESMERALDA:
And, oh, God, let me dream tonight of the Chosen Hero!

GYPSY:
Now, sleep. Fly away on the magic carpet of dreams!

[*Esmeralda crawls into the gauze-tented cot. The Gypsy descends from the roof.*]

KILROY:
Esmeralda! My little Gypsy sweetheart!

ESMERALDA [*sleepily*]:
Go away, cat.

[*The light behind the gauze is gradually dimming.*]

KILROY:
This is no cat. This is the chosen hero of the big fiesta, Kilroy,

the champion of the golden gloves with his gold heart cut from his chest and in his hands to give you!

ESMERALDA:

Go away. Let me dream of the Chosen Hero.

KILROY:

What a hassle! Mistook for a cat! What can I do to convince this doll I'm real?

[*Three brass balls wink brilliantly.*]

—Another transaction seems to be indicated!

[*He rushes to the Loan Shark's. The entrance immediately lights up.*]

My heart is gold! What will you give me for it?

[*Jewels, furs, sequined gowns, etc., are tossed to his feet. He throws his heart like a basketball to the Loan Shark, snatches up the loot and rushes back to the Gypsy's.*]

Doll! Behold this loot! I gave my golden heart for it!

ESMERALDA:

Go away, cat . . .

[*She falls asleep. Kilroy bangs his forehead with his fist, then rushes to the Gypsy's door, pounds it with both fists. The door is thrown open and the sordid contents of a large jar are thrown at him. He falls back gasping, spluttering, retching. He retreats and finally assumes an exaggerated attitude of despair.*]

KILROY:

Had for a button! Stewed, screwed and tattooed on the Camino Real! Baptized, finally, with the contents of a slop-jar!—Did anybody say the deal was rugged?!

157

[*Quixote stirs against the wall of Skid Row. He hawks and spits and staggers to his feet.*]

GUTMAN:

Why, the old knight's awake, his dream is over!

QUIXOTE [*to Kilroy*]:

Hello! Is that a fountain?

KILROY:

—Yeah, but—

QUIXOTE:

I've got a mouthful of old chicken feathers . . .

[*He approaches the fountain. It begins to flow. Kilroy falls back in amazement as the Old Knight rinses his mouth and drinks and removes his jacket to bathe, handing the tattered garment to Kilroy.*]

QUIXOTE [*as he bathes*]:

Qué pasa, mi amigo?

KILROY:

The deal is rugged. D'you know what I mean?

QUIXOTE:

Who knows better than I what a rugged deal is!

[*He produces a toothbrush and brushes his teeth.*]

—Will you take some advice?

KILROY:

Brother, at this point on the Camino I will take anything which is offered!

QUIXOTE:

Don't! Pity! Your! Self!

158

[*He takes out a pocket mirror and grooms his beard and moustache.*]

The wounds of the vanity, the many offenses our egos have to endure, being housed in bodies that age and hearts that grow tired, are better accepted with a tolerant smile—like *this!* —You *see?*

[*He cracks his face in two with an enormous grin.*]

GUTMAN:
Follow-spot on the face of the ancient knight!

QUIXOTE:
Otherwise what you become is a bag full of curdled cream— *leche mala,* we call it!—attractive to nobody, least of all to yourself!

[*He passes the comb and pocket mirror to Kilroy.*]

Have you got any plans?

KILROY [*a bit uncertainly, wistfully*]:
Well, I was thinking of—going *on* from—*here!*

QUIXOTE:
Good! Come with me.

KILROY [*to the audience*]:
Crazy old bastard.

[*Then to the Knight:*]

Donde?

QUIXOTE [*starting for the stairs*]:
Quien sabe!

[*The fountain is now flowing loudly and sweetly. The Street People are moving toward it with murmurs of wonder. Marguerite comes out upon the terrace.*]

159

KILROY:

Hey, there's—!

QUIXOTE:

Shhh! Listen!

[*They pause on the stairs.*]

MARGUERITE:

Abdullah!

[*Gutman has descended to the terrace.*]

GUTMAN:

Mademoiselle, allow me to deliver the message for you. It would be in bad form if I didn't take some final part in the pageant.

[*He crosses the plaza to the opposite façade and shouts "Casanova!" under the window of the "Ritz Men Only."*

[*Meanwhile Kilroy scratches out the verb "is" and prints the correction "was" in the inscription on the ancient wall.*]

Casanova! Great lover and King of Cuckolds on the Camino Real! The last of your ladies has guaranteed your tabs and is expecting you for breakfast on the terrace!

[*Casanova looks first out of the practical window of the flophouse, then emerges from its scabrous doorway, haggard, unshaven, crumpled in dress but bearing himself as erectly as ever. He blinks and glares fiercely into the brilliant morning light.*

[*Marguerite cannot return his look, she averts her face with a look for which anguish would not be too strong a term, but at the same time she extends a pleading hand toward him. After some hesitation, he begins to move toward her,*

160

striking the pavement in measured cadence with his cane, glancing once, as he crosses, out at the audience with a wry smile that makes admissions that would be embarrassing to a vainer man than Casanova now is. When he reaches Marguerite she gropes for his hand, seizes it with a low cry and presses it spasmodically to her lips while he draws her into his arms and looks above her sobbing, dyed-golden head with the serene, clouded gaze of someone mortally ill as the mercy of a narcotic laps over his pain.

[*Quixote raises his lance in a formal gesture and cries out hoarsely, powerfully from the stairs:*]

QUIXOTE:
The violets in the mountains have broken the rocks!

[*Quixote goes through the arch with Kilroy.*]

GUTMAN [*to the audience*]:
The Curtain Line has been spoken!

[*To the wings:*]

Bring it down!

[*He bows with a fat man's grace as—*

[*The curtain falls.*]